olm
10-10

Evagrius Ponticus
and Cognitive Science

Evagrius Ponticus
and Cognitive Science

A Look at Moral Evil and the Thoughts

GEORGE TSAKIRIDIS

PICKWICK *Publications* · Eugene, Oregon

EVAGRIUS PONTICUS AND COGNITIVE SCIENCE
A Look at Moral Evil and the Thoughts

Pickwick Publications
An Imprint of Wipf and Stock Publishers
199 W. 8th Ave., Suite 3
Eugene, OR 97401

www.wipfandstock.com

ISBN 13: 978-1-60899-066-5

Cataloguing-in-Publication data:

Tsakiridis, George

    Evagrius Ponticus and cognitive science : a look at moral evil and the thoughts /
George Tsakiridis

    xii + 124 p. ; 23 cm. Includes bibliographical references.

    ISBN 13: 978-1-60899-066-5

    1. Evagrius, Ponticus, 345?–399. 2. Cognitive science. 3. Good and evil. I. Title.

BR65.E93 T77 2010

Manufactured in the U.S.A.

To Baby Tsakiridis

You were loved, you will be missed

Contents

Acknowledgments

WHEN UNDERTAKING A PROJECT of this breadth, many people are involved in its completion. I would not have been able to finish this book without the help and support of professors, family, and friends. Before moving into the actual text of this volume, I would like to take this opportunity to thank them.

First, I would like to thank my wife, Jocelyn. Without her support the completion of this project would have been many times more difficult. She did many things, not least among them cooking me nutritious and tasty meals, which sustained my health. She has been my best friend through this endeavor. She is to be commended for keeping me sane, especially due to the pace at which I worked through the last two years of my dissertation.

Next I would like to thank my parents, Christos and Dorcas. Without their support I would not have been able to complete as much schooling as I have. They have been loving and dependable parents, something that is becoming increasingly rare. I would also like to thank my now deceased grandfather, George L. George, who was a constant support. I am glad to have been able to move back to Chicago for the last leg of my schooling in order to spend time with him before he passed on.

I also owe much to Robert Cathey, my advisor. He has been organized, supportive, and helpful through the whole process. Dr. Cathey allowed the project to unfold organically, without forcing me to abandon my interests and strengths. Bob was there to lead me through the difficult reality of an advisor change, and I am incredibly grateful. Enough cannot be said about his influence.

I also must thank the rest of my dissertation committee, John Albright, José David Rodríguez, and Mark Swanson, who all brought individual strengths and insights that were invaluable. I have known John Albright for quite a while, and he has been a support throughout my whole program, and a helpful influence since I met him at the AAR national meeting back in November of 2000. José David Rodríguez does not get enough credit for the work he does and I want him to know that I do realize how much he has humbly done behind the scenes to make this project a reality. Mark Swanson was a constant source of input and without his expertise on Evagrius Ponticus this project would never have taken place. I was fortunate to have such a competent and supportive committee.

In addition, both Joe Gaston and Tiffany Demke are owed thanks for their help in allowing me to discuss this project with them both professionally and as friends. Joe was the respondent at the public presentation of my proposal for this project and has been a good friend. I have known Tiffany since we both started doctoral work in 2003, and have appreciated her friendship.

I would also like to thank Jim Schaal, the executive coordinator at the Zygon Center for Religion and Science, who was always a friendly source of discussion, as well as everyone at the Zygon Center for their support over the years. In addition, let me also offer my thanks to Bruce Beck at the Pappas Patristic Institute, Father Elijah Mueller, and Rebecca Luft, who all contributed to my knowledge of patristics and helped in various ways on this project. I also want to thank Tom Johnson and Patrick Bennett of the Indiana State University Center for the Study of Health, Religion, and Spirituality, as well as Kenneth Pargament, who all contributed to making this a stronger volume in the area of psychology.

Lastly, I would like to thank Wipf & Stock Publishers for taking this project to press and allowing me to share my writings with a broader audience. I am thankful for this opportunity. I am sure there are many others who deserve thanks, but for the sake of space, I will stop at these. Thanks to all of you.

A FEW YEARS AGO I was struggling with what to write on for my dissertation topic. I had a great interest in sin, but didn't know if it would be the right topic for a dissertation in religion and science with where I was headed in my scholastic career. I went through various iterations of topics ranging from truth to atonement, but did not find something that fully engaged me. It was through the television show *Highlander* that I finally decided that I wanted to write about evil. Sin and evil have always been of great interest to me, whatever that says about me personally. Perhaps this is because it is second nature to all of us—or should I say "first nature." X Anyway, I was watching the last episode of season 5 and the first 2 episodes of season 6, which engage mythical evil in the world of immortals. It was at this point that I realized I would enjoy going this route in my scholarship. No matter how much I try to get away from the study of sin or evil, it seems to always beckon me back, and rightfully so. This book is an edited version of my original dissertation, so, as a disclaimer, it does have the trappings of a dissertation.

This particular study engages some of my greatest intellectual interests: patristics, sin and evil, and the sciences. It also is personally dear to me because Evagrius is from Pontus, where some of my own ancestry resides. I am fortunate that the stars aligned in this way, or—for Calvinists—that the providence of God saw fit to allow these diverse areas of study to come together in this project. Because of the interdisciplinary nature of the book, there will probably be sections that are unfamiliar to some readers, but this is part of the difficulty in any dialogue between religion and science. I have done my best to make the text accessible, while still staying in an academic genre that assumes some knowledge in academic theology.

Patristics is a foundational part of Christian theology and I feel it my duty to bring it into dialogue with the sciences, first, because it is relevant to theology and science dialogue, but second, and primarily, because I enjoy both areas of study and would hate to leave either behind.

As regards Evagrius Ponticus, he is a timely figure in patristic studies due to the most recent scholarship on his writings. Ten years ago this volume would have taken years longer to write and been severely limited by the available English scholarship. Today there are a wealth of books coming out on Evagrius, and I am a part of the early stages of this restoration. He may not ever be canonized, but his work is more broadly known than it was even five to ten years ago.

In this same way, the cognitive sciences are a burgeoning field. There is quite a bit written, but so much unknown. I can definitely foresee future scholarship building on this volume, but also engaging its limitations, as more and more scientific discovery is revealed in the area of brain science. At the same time, we must do with what we have, and this study opens a dialogue that I think will continue for years to come.

So of what use is this text? Evagrian scholars will be interested in this study for obvious reasons. One positive (and negative) aspect of studies on Evagrius Ponticus is that the corpus of writings is still limited. Even with the recent growth of scholarship, there are a manageable number of texts to read. It is my hope that the broader religion and science community will also take interest in this study, not only because of the particulars of this research, but also for the larger implications on how we view moral evil and spirituality. It is this view to evil and spirituality to which this book appeals. Understanding evil is a pursuit that is millennia old, but never seems to present satisfactory answers. This text tries to put forth some practical descriptions of how to combat evil, while also attempting to grasp the theoretical concept of evil. Both the Christian and the non-Christian can appropriate the results as they will, but the lines of dialogue that are opened in the following pages are of use to those who wonder about supernatural language and related categories.

It is without delay, then, that I leave you with these brief words and I hope that you enjoy the dialogue between the many voices presented. It is only a beginning, and I realize that I am concise at times where more can be said, but sometimes brevity is preferable and more practical. I believe this is appropriate for a text calling for the practical appropriation of theoretical scholarship.

ONE

Introduction

FROM THE BEGINNINGS OF Christianity one wonders why a good God would allow evil to exist, even more why a good God would create evil. In recent years, science has helped us to understand evil in ways previously untapped. Although these questions of theodicy are still important in our day, there is a deeper, more theologically relevant question underlying this: "What is evil for the human person?" If one does not know what evil is, how is it possible to discuss its existence intelligibly in relation to a good God? This particular study will delve into a facet of this question, using one Eastern patristic thinker's ideas on sin and evil, a philosophic theology of evil, and modern cognitive science as it relates to evil and prayer. This study will show how Evagrius Ponticus' conception of evil thoughts and their remedies, one of which is prayer, is relevant today within a context of cognitive science and its relation to meditation and prayer. It will also show how Evagrius defines evil thoughts, working predominately in the mind, moving toward a dialogical discussion with cognitive science. In this way, the questions "What is (moral) evil?" and "How does one personally overcome (moral) evil?" are at the fore of this study.

This study is addressed predominately to the Christian, who, despite confessional beliefs, still holds science in high regard and has some doubt as to the validity of supernatural language regarding demons and angels. In addition, mysticism will be a part of this study, which will show that there is some empirical evidence for mystic experience. Relationship with

1

God is one of the ultimate foundations of Christianity, and for some this may take the form of mystic experience. In most mainline Protestant denominations, this sort of relationship is looked at skeptically, and with some reasonable cause. Because mystic experiences, as well as most supernatural experiences, are personal, they are hard to verify and thus are viewed questionably. The Enlightenment has created a level of doubt that must be overcome, although in many cases this doubt helps us to sift through the pretenders and charlatans. Again, this study is not meant to focus on mysticism, although that is a part of it. The supernatural has become suspect due to this sort of Enlightenment approach, despite the fact that Christianity is founded on a supernatural event: the resurrection of Jesus Christ. Thus, discussion of thoughts, demons, angels, and prayer in Evagrius should not be viewed as strange, despite their distance from the world of mainline Protestant Christianity. Anxiety and moral evil are shown to be combated by prayer and Scripture in Evagrius, and can still be combated in like manner today. It is my hope that this study will offer optimism to those who, in addition to their confessional, relational faith, still look to the scientific world for some answers.

This study is divided into five chapters, including this introduction. The second chapter is a discussion of Evagrius Ponticus—his life and thought. It will present Evagrius' arguments in regard to evil and the "thoughts." His use of the eight thoughts is pertinent for dialogue about evil in the mind.[1] The fourth-century monastic prescriptions for addressing this "evil" are still theologically significant today. This section will not focus on his biography, but a brief overview of his life may be helpful in showing his context. The third chapter will present a philosophical/historical discussion of evil, focusing in large part on Paul Ricoeur's work on evil, and also on the work of Pierre Hadot, a scholar who has helped to interpret ancient writers in a contemporary light while respecting their historical context. The fourth chapter will discuss contemporary cognitive science and how research in this field is working with conceptions of evil in the mind. Meditation and prayer are on the opposite side of this discussion and relevant in creating a dialogue with Evagrius. Work in cognitive science is being done on both sides of this issue and in related

1. In this study I will typically not place "thoughts" or "eight thoughts" within quotation marks unless appropriate. Evagrius referenced the eight thoughts or thoughts in multiple works, and the term "eight thoughts" does not necessarily refer to one specific work of his.

ways. This brings us to the fifth and final chapter, which will integrate the previous three, working principally with a comparison of Evagrius' work and modern cognitive science. By using the lens of Ricoeur and Hadot, we will be able to create a dialogical approach to moral evil using Evagrius' thoughts, philosophy, and cognitive science.

Ultimately the goal of this study is apologetic in nature. Although I dislike using that word at times because of its pejorative use by some scholars, much of the work done in theology is apologetic. Making an argument to defend underlying beliefs and principles is prevalent in most areas of scholarship. In this study, I am attempting to defend both supernatural language and the orthodox Christian faith without being shortsighted on either count. The argument I make is in large part analogical, in part out of necessity due to the historical gap, and in part because of my own proclivity for analogy. Using Evagrius and the cognitive sciences, I am able to connect his own views on evil and prayer to current research in brain science. Thus, some empirical support is offered for Evagrius' work and orthodox Christian spirituality in general, both Eastern Orthodox and Western.

Evagrius and the Eight Thoughts: Evil and Prayer

Evagrius Ponticus was born in about 345 CE in Ibora, Pontus.[2] His life overlapped and interacted with many of the great thinkers of Eastern patristic thought, which any study of his life will show.[3] He was trained by the Cappadocian Fathers, which is of importance in exploring his thought. Although I will move forward without recounting his life, it is worth noting that Evagrius holds a somewhat tenuous place in church history due to his entanglements with Origen's thought.

Given his background as a monastic and a fourth-century thinker, one of Evagrius' great contributions to theological scholarship is his concept of the "thoughts." He presented eight different thoughts (in more than one of his works), and this set the groundwork for the seven

λογισμοί

2. Casiday, *Evagrius Ponticus*, 6. I will be referring to Evagrius Ponticus as Evagrius, but it is worth noting that there was a later Evagrius, Evagrius Scholasticus.

3. Ibid., 5–13. It is clear that Evagrius had relationships with Basil the Great, Gregory Nazianzen, and Macarius the Great as well as others. One can see this specifically on pages 6, 7, and 10.

deadly sins of Gregory the Great.[4] The thoughts are: gluttony, fornication, avarice, anger, sadness, acedia, vainglory, and pride.[5] In reading Evagrius, it is clear that he holds to a viewpoint that might be expected of a fourth-century monk. These "demons"—another term used for the thoughts—are outer forces that work upon the monk's mind.[6] These must be countered by various practices, including prayer. In his work *To Eulogios. On the Confession of Thoughts and Counsel in Their Regard*, this is made explicit: "The demons make war on the soul by means of thoughts and they are countered in turn with a more difficult warfare by means of perseverance . . . ."[7] Earlier in this same work he states, "In the laziness

4. Stewart, *Cassian the Monk*, 179n23.

5. Evagrius *On the Eight Thoughts* (Evagrius, *Evagrius of Pontus*, 73–90).

6. It is worth noting here, and will be pertinent again later, that the concept of mind has many uses and is contrasted with the brain in cognitive science literature. When one speaks of mind, this often is not clearly defined, but here it is generally referring to the emergent consciousness that arises from biological matter, i.e., the brain. Below I provide working definitions of this and other key concepts:

Evil— A descriptive term used to describe something as destructive or hurtful, but in an extreme way. This is brought out in the way that evil actually is described as an entity of its own. Some see it as an actual being, some as nothingness. Karl Barth, for example, holds this view of nothingness (Schwarz, *Evil*, 163–68). In regard to the mind, evil can be described as thoughts that are destructive to the self or the other. Hence all evil that comes from humanity emerges from the mind initially. The thought can be seen as evil in itself or can lead to evil action. I am describing it as such as it will be important for Evagrius and this book. Evagrius' use of "thoughts" will become clear in chapter 2.

Brain— The biological organ that is the origin of thought for a person. This term refers only to the biological entity itself.

Mind— The emergent consciousness that arises out of a person's brain. This is where the personality, thought process, etc. are located. It does not have a physical form. When discussing both mind and soul in opposition to body (and brain) some will question whether there is a dualistic nature to humanity. There is still much debate over the idea of emergence in regard to mind.

Soul— The immaterial part of a person, which also could be seen as one's mind, especially in older theological literature. Traditionally, it is the part of a person that survives death. It goes beyond mind in that it usually does not only refer to the consciousness, but to the immaterial self.

Will— The decision-making consciousness in the mind. The will is also an emergent function of the brain.

Also worth noting is that Sinkewicz makes a point to state that "for Evagrius the terms 'thoughts' . . . and 'fantasies' . . . took on a strongly negative cast, with the latter term bearing much of its modern psychological connotations." Sinkewicz in Evagrius, *Evagrius of Pontus*, xxv.

7. Evagrius *To Eulogios* 15 (*Evagrius of Pontus*, 42). "Soul" is used in such a way that it can also refer to mind, as the previous note alludes to—the transcendent self.

[Handwritten marginalia: "Glossary"; "there is no 'evil' in itself"; "Evil is a perversion or deviation from the good or God's will"; "Evagrius doesn't feel this"; "NOUS"]

of the soul the demons are able to get hold of our rational mind and in the thoughts they disgorge the pleasures of evil."[8] In addition to this, in the *Praktikos* he follows the eight evil thoughts with eight corresponding remedies.[9] There are countless other examples of this approach to evil and the thoughts, although Evagrius sees evil working in thought more for the holy one than for the secular. Further on in *Praktikos* he states, "The demons war with seculars more through objects, but with monks they do so especially through thoughts, for they are deprived of objects because of the solitude."[10] In fact, he even references the brain stem being manipulated by deceptive forms of prayer, a reference to both a physical and spiritual reality in a part of the brain.[11] Given the time period, it is clear that he did not view the "brain" in the same way a cognitive scientist of the twenty-first century would, but this still raises a relevant point about the language Evagrius uses. "Mind," "brain," "soul" and other descriptive nouns are all used with reference to the way demons affect the thoughts of the pious one.

Note that, for purposes of discussing Evagrius, "mind" and "soul" may be somewhat interchangeable, with these terms referring to the transcendent quality that emerges from a human body.[12] In his writings, there is a clear connection between evil, the mind, and prayer. This will be expanded upon as this study moves forward, but it should be apparent how this discussion will yield fruit in dialogue with current scholarship in cognitive science. The study of Evagrius is especially profitable in that this line of thought is located in many of his writings, presenting a worldview that places evil and the demonic in opposition to prayer and the holy.

A word about footnotes citing Evagrius: first the original Evagrius text is cited, followed in parentheses by the source text in which the translation is found. Where the source text is listed in the bibliography under Evagrius, only the title and page reference are given. Where applicable, "ibid." is used in parentheses to refer to the source text cited in the preceding footnote, even where the notes refer to different Evagrius texts (see the following 3 footnotes).

8. *To Eulogios* 13 (ibid., 39).

9. Evagrius *Praktikos* 15–33 (ibid., 100–103).

10. *Praktikos* 48 (ibid., 106).

11. Stewart, "Practices of Monastic Prayer," 9, 17; referencing Evagrius *On Prayer* 72–73 (*Evagrius of Pontus*, 200–201). Note that Stewart refers to these 2 chapters of *On Prayer* as 73–74, as they are numbered in Casiday, *Evagrius Ponticus*, 193–94.

12. I am using "emerges" as my own term. Also refer back to the working definitions of relevant terms in note 6 above.

A Discussion of Evil and a Recovery of Evagrius

Chapter 3 opens with a broader discussion of evil, presenting maxims that are helpful for laying out theological boundaries for a discussion of evil in Christian theology. Evil may be best described by stating what one can know about it, in part due to the fact that it is so difficult to define.

Following this discussion, the work of Pierre Hadot shows us how Evagrius is linked to ancient philosophical sources, as well as how one recovers the meaning of ancient sources into a modern context. Hadot states, "Opening these old books, then, the modern reader has to be extremely careful. We run the constant risk of mistaking a schoolroom commonplace for a revelatory detail."[13] We must look at ancient texts with a different lens. What seems notable to modern readers may be mundane for the writer.[14] This is depicted more explicitly in Hadot's *Philosophy as a Way of Life*. He gives numerous examples of what was important to the ancients, first among them meditation. Speaking of the Greco-Roman world, he states, "The relationship between theory and practice in the philosophy of this period must be understood from the perspective of these exercises of meditation."[15] He also notes adeptly that most of the Hellenistic philosophy of ancient times has been lost; thus history paints a different picture than what actually transpired.[16] Of special note is the reference that Hadot makes to Evagrius.[17] He states that Evagrius mirrors Plato and Zeno in stating that "the quality of our dreams allows us to judge the spiritual state of our soul."[18] He also states that Evagrius' use of one thought to combat another can be seen in Cicero in *Tusculan Disputations*.[19] Evagrius, as a learned man, may be drawing on Greek philosophy in his approach, and in fact, given what we know, it would be strange if he was not. It is clear that Hadot's work is of great use in both placing Evagrius in context and interpreting his writings.

Following a discussion of Hadot, the work of Paul Ricoeur is of prime importance because his work on the symbols of evil provides a founda-

---

13. Hadot, *Plotinus*, 18.

14. Ibid.

15. Hadot, *Philosophy as a Way of Life*, 60; see 59–60.

16. Ibid., 53.

17. Ibid., numerous times in 133–38.

18. Ibid., 135.

19. Ibid.

tion for a later discussion of myth and symbol in the cognitive sciences on the subject of good and evil.[20] Ricoeur discusses the symbols of evil, and works through a discussion of myth related to evil. Early on he discusses guilt as pointing to "a more fundamental experience, the experience of 'sin,' which includes *all* men and indicates the *real* situation of man before God, whether man knows it or not." A bit earlier he states, "Language is the light of the emotions."[21] In this we see Ricoeur speaking of making the unspoken spoken, and thought becoming language. This is reminiscent of Evagrius' talk of demons attacking the secular person through objects, but the monk through thoughts.[22] Evagrius and Ricoeur speak of "thought" in two different senses. Ricoeur means thought arising out of the fundamental symbol, while Evagrius means thought in an external sense, as in a demon or thought approaching the monk from the outside. The common language that is used, however, opens up ground for dialogue, despite this fundamental difference in the usage. In *The Symbolism of Evil*, Ricoeur goes on to trace the symbols of evil, from defilement to sin to guilt (in part 1, chapters 1–3), and, in a similar fashion to Evagrius, Ricoeur starts with the outer (defilement) and moves to the inner (guilt). Evagrius does the same thing as he moves from the practices (the outer actions) to pure prayer (the inner, and utmost action).[23] This parallel is striking, and one of the most useful connections between these two authors. Ricoeur's discussion of the four types of myth (in part 2, chapters 1–4)—creation and chaos, tragic, Adamic, and that of the exiled soul—is also relevant as these myths connect ancient history/philosophy with Christian theology. Ricoeur's work presenting a history of the symbols and myths of evil is also useful in linking to how cognitive science shows that the brain forms myth. Ricoeur thus works as an intermediary for Evagrius, evil, and myth formation in cognitive science to bring us into the twenty-first century.[24]

20. *Symbolism of Evil* is Ricoeur's chief work on this topic.

21. Ibid., 7.

22. *Praktikos* 48 (Evagrius, *Evagrius of Pontus*, 106).

23. See Stewart, "Imageless Prayer," 178; and Bamberger in his introduction in Evagrius, *Praktikos*, xc–xci.

24. Also useful in the discussion of Evagrius' context and for a theological/philosophical discussion of evil are: Jaroslav Pelikan, *Christianity and Classical Culture*; Hans Schwarz, *Evil: A Historical and Theological Perspective*; and Terry D. Cooper, *Dimensions of Evil*.

How the Mind Deals with Evil: Cognitive Science

Once we have established means with which to read Evagrius' fourth-century view of evil, and the mythical/symbolic development as a foundation of evil for Christian theology, it will be possible to look at sin and evil through the eyes of cognitive science. This will also lead us to a discussion on prayer, meditation, and spirituality as a prescription for evil. Chapter 4 of this study opens with a discussion of the work of William James. His writings help to build a bridge from philosophy to the cognitive sciences.[25]

Following this discussion will be a section on evil and the brain. When looking inside the realm of cognitive science, there are many directions in which one can see avenues for the discussion of sin and evil. One major question that comes to prominence is, "In dealing with the human mind, what is evil?" In other words, is evil something that is created from within the mind? Is it an external force exerted on the mind? Or is it only defined in relation to other human beings and their actions? For the moment, let us leave behind the idea of natural evil and focus on the cognitive source of evil or evil thoughts. This has manifestation in the physical realm, but how? Is it in the way the brain is affected? Or in the evil actions that follow from the original thought? Within the realm of cognitive science, the question can be addressed in multiple ways. First, in looking at the work of d'Aquili and Newberg, they have proposed a system of operators, among them the binary operator, which allows humans to divide elements into polar opposites, for example good and evil.[26] This is helpful for seeing the need to categorize good and evil. Second, for the mind, what is sin? Is socialization a part of this process in defining what is good and what is evil? Related to this is how stress and anxiety in the mind can lead to various actions and physical effects within the brain. It is worth noting that the mind/brain divide is an important one when thinking about sin and evil.

Drawing on the discussion of evil from the previous chapter, we will see that Ricoeur's symbolism of evil is relevant in a discussion of d'Aquili and Newberg's binary operator. The myth-making part of this function

---

25. This section focuses on James, *Varieties of Religious Experience*, 15–16. These pages bring to light his discussion on "medical materialism." Lecture 1 ("Religion and Neurology"), and lectures 16 and 17 ("Mysticism") are also relevant (ibid.).

26. d'Aquili and Newberg, *Mystical Mind*, 55.

dialogues well with Ricoeur's symbolism and the myths it produces. It is also worth noting that Ricoeur has co-written a book titled *What Makes Us Think?* with Jean-Pierre Changeux, a neuroscientist, in which there is a running dialogue between the two, allowing us to build on Ricoeur's philosophy of evil and how this works with modern cognitive science. This additional, direct dialogue gives an insight into some of the key questions for the philosopher in addressing cognitive science. Along these lines, according to d'Aquili and Newberg, the binary operator "allows us to extract meaning from the external world by ordering abstract elements into dyads. A dyad is a group of two elements that are opposed to each other in their meaning . . . good and evil, right and wrong."[27] They go on to state that this is important in the formation of myth. The authors discuss further how the mind's operators influence the formation of myth, something that will be explored more in the fourth chapter.[28]

In addition, external factors play a role in how the brain perceives good and evil. This is related to anxiety and its affect on how the mind reacts to various inputs. Some actions may flow out of a perceived good, when in fact those actions are destructive. Anxiety and stress cause the mind to act in a different manner than under "normal" conditions. This is what James Ashbrook and Carol Albright refer to as "The Defense System" for the brain. Under stressful conditions the body acts in a different mode to protect itself. This mode can cause decisions that may result in "evil" actions coming from a misperception of reality. As Ashbrook and Albright describe it, "To make the best decisions, all parts of the brain must contribute to perception, classification, and understanding of situations. . . . Malicious behavior thus arises out of a misguided effort at self-preservation."[29] They go on to state that this behavior may be on a one-to-one basis or in a societal structure.[30] This idea of the "malfunctioning" brain is a key element in the discussion of evil in the mind. It

27. Ibid.

28. Ibid. They explicitly explore myth in chapter 4 of *The Mystical Mind*.

29. Quotations from Ashbrook and Albright, *Humanizing Brain*, 159, 160. This text was also published as *Where God Lives in the Human Brain*, but for this study I have chosen to use the former title.

30. Ibid. The concepts from this paragraph (the third point) can be found in ibid., 156–61. The discussion of societal evil on p. 160 may link back to Reinhold Niebuhr's work in a fruitful manner. "The Defense System" is explained on pp. 158–61, with a descriptive table on p. 159.

also leads to an "antidote," which can be prayer, meditation, and other spiritual exercises.

While holding off on comparisons to Evagrius' work until the final chapter, it is important to note the work being done in the cognitive sciences in regard to meditation, prayer, and spirituality. The next section of chapter 4 will address these issues. Kenneth Pargament has done research showing that psychological treatment works better when a spiritual dimension is offered, as opposed to just a psychological one. Another example of work addressing the effect of meditation and prayer on the brain is found in the work of d'Aquili and Newberg (with Vince Rause) in their book *Why God Won't Go Away*. Here they show how meditation has an effect on blood flow in the brain. Although this approach is still in the early stages of empirical research, it shows that meditation has a tangible effect on the brain.

In Pargament's book *Spiritually Integrated Psychotherapy*, he addresses the question of whether spiritually integrated psychotherapy works.[31] Although the research is still in the beginning stages, there is reason to believe that therapy is more effective for those who integrate a spiritual dimension with it, but this may also depend on the patient's own spiritual proclivities.[32]

Continuing to look at how spirituality affects the brain, in *Why God Won't Go Away* the authors describe how observation of Buddhist monks meditating and Franciscan nuns praying show tangible change in the brain. They state:

> As our study continued, and the data flowed in, Gene and I suspected that we'd uncovered solid evidence that the mystical experiences of our subjects—the altered states of mind they described as the absorption of the self into something larger—were not the result of emotional mistakes or simple wishful thinking, but were associated instead with a series of observable neurological events, which, while unusual, are not outside the range of normal brain function. In other words, mystical experience is biologically, observably, and scientifically real.[33]

31. Pargament, *Spiritually Integrated Psychotherapy*, 325–26.

32. Ibid., 320, 326–28.

33. d'Aquili, Newberg, and Rause, *Why God Won't Go Away*, 7.

Again, the results are limited, but hopeful, in demonstrating that prayer and meditation have a biological effect on the brain, shown in blood movement, and a positive effect on the mind, shown in psychological recovery.

This section presents the four major theses for cognitive science that appear in this book. First, there are mind/brain structures in place that cause human beings to construct myths including the dyad of good and evil. Second, the brain/mind perceives evil in different ways depending on its health. Third, the evil experienced by the mind can be treated by prayer, meditation, and psychotherapy with a spiritual component. Fourth, meditation and prayer can be observed to have a physical effect on the brain, showing there is empirical evidence of meditative effects. Both the physical component (brain) and consciousness (mind) are important to this discussion.

A Synthesis of Evagrius and Cognitive Science: Constructing a View of Evil

The final chapter synthesizes the previous three chapters, mainly focusing on the second and the fourth chapter, and using the third as a bridge through which to evoke dialogue. I show, using the research of cognitive science and the work of Evagrius, that moral evil is indeed operative in the mind in unhealthy thought, and can be countered by prayer. This final chapter opens with a discussion on Orthodox psychotherapy, followed by this synthesis, which will then lead to a section that constructs a dialogical approach to discussing evil.

It should be evident that there are many connection points between Evagrius' fourth-century writing and modern research in the field of cognitive science. Evagrius presents evil/sin in the mind and thoughts as a force that is both exterior and interior. He combines both the internal sinfulness of humanity and the external, supernatural demonic. To counter this, both internal and external counter-forces must be used: monastic discipline and the power of God. Evagrius' approach to pure prayer and the movement from external practice to internal prayer adds additional layers of interest. The light seen in pure prayer may be investigated to see if cognitive science tells us what this might be. In regard to the move from the external to the internal, this might be seen to parallel Ricoeur's approach to the symbols of evil, and hence add not only a component of moral evil, but also one of inherent evil in the human thought process.

This helps to link Evagrius, Ricoeur, and cognitive science in one line of thought, shown in an external-to-internal move in formation of both a myth of evil and an approach to combat moral evil.

As we move into the present day, philosophical conceptions of evil, notably those of Ricoeur, show that myth, symbol, and thought are major themes in building a theory of evil. The work of Pierre Hadot will allow modern readers to hear Evagrius "correctly," avoiding anachronisms that would otherwise be present. This leads us into dialogue with cognitive science, where myth formation is a primary concept.

In the context of cognitive science, one sees that myth is a function of the brain, and evil actions can be seen as an attempt at wellbeing from the standpoint of the brain when under anxiety. As with Evagrius, this can be countered by meditation and prayer. Recent research is showing that in treatment of the mind, a component of spirituality is beneficial. In addition, as d'Aquili and Newberg have shown, there is a physical change in the brain during meditation, although the results are still limited in scope.

When looking at the breadth of this study, we see that Evagrius' monastic admonitions regarding the thoughts and prayer are quite applicable to the present day, as they can be drawn into dialogue with research in the cognitive sciences. As this study unfolds, the details will become clearer, showing that Evagrian conceptions of the thoughts and prayer may have many parallels with modern cognitive science. Even in this introductory look, it is evident that this will be a fruitful endeavor.

To summarize, the approach I am taking is as follows:

1. To read Evagrius Ponticus on evil and the thoughts, taking into account his prescriptions for combating evil

2. To use Pierre Hadot and Paul Ricoeur (as well as others to a lesser degree) to recover Evagrius' contextual meaning and show the formation of evil from a Christian theological/philosophical standpoint

3. To present modern cognitive science views on moral evil in the brain/ mind and myth formation of evil

4. To show that Evagrius' prescriptions are still relevant in light of modern cognitive science and psychotherapy

This book breaks new ground in systematic theology for a few different reasons. First, to my knowledge, it is the first work that has dealt exclusively with Evagrius and modern cognitive science. Typically, Eastern patristic thinkers are not placed into dialogue with science, so it is unique on that count. In this realm, some may question whether the appropriation of Evagrius' eight thoughts is a legitimate endeavor. I would point to the precedent set by Cassian and Gregory the Great in short order after the time of Evagrius.[34] Just as they appropriated his work for Western theologians, I am using his work to engage the sciences and Western theology. Second, I am placing Evagrius into dialogue with Ricoeur and some modern theological thought. Evagrian studies have seen a resurgence in the past fifty years, and especially in the last ten. He has not had a chance to dialogue with some of these new partners. Third, I am observing Evagrius from the point of view of a practical theological approach, in addition to a systematic, modern approach. I do not know of any work that combines the practical words of Evagrius with the practical and technical approach to spirituality in cognitive science/psychotherapy. This study has roots in both the practical and the theoretical, which are ultimately two of the major worlds that I am bringing together.

34. Stewart, *Cassian the Monk*, 179n23.

two

Evagrius and the Eight Thoughts

Evil and Prayer

EVAGRIUS PONTICUS IS SOMETHING of a lost figure in patristic discussions, in large part due to the continued acceptance of his condemnation in 553 at the Council of Constantinople for disseminating
a metaphysics deemed heretical.[1] Although known to many, he still has
not achieved mainstream acceptance, at least in the Western church. This
chapter will focus predominately on his discussion of the eight thoughts,
their remedies, and how they can be used in a discussion on evil in the
mind. In order to better understand the man and the context in which his
writings are rooted, it is necessary to present a brief biography, showing
the relevance of the eight thoughts to the study at hand.

Biography of Evagrius Ponticus and Introduction to the Thoughts

1. *Biography and Definitions*

Evagrius was born in approximately 345 CE in Ibora, Pontus.[2] He was
the son of a chorbishop (a bishop with limited powers of exercise) in a

1. Casiday, "Gabriel Bunge," 249–50; and Clark, *Origenist Controversy*, 249. Clark
discusses Evagrius' Origenism in part.

2. Casiday, *Evagrius Ponticus*, 6.

rural area. He grew up close to the family estate of Basil the Great, and it was Basil who ordained him as a lector.[3] He later became a deacon under Gregory Nazianzen after Basil died, before moving on to Jerusalem. The reason for the move to Jerusalem was an affair with a married woman. In a vision, he was incarcerated and subsequently warned by an angel to leave the city of Constantinople. This prompted him to get on a ship to Jerusalem, most likely in 382. There he spent time with Melania the Elder. During this period he was stricken with a six-month illness, seemingly brought on by his own sin. When Melania became aware of this, she forced him to promise to become a monk. He was healed soon after this promise and went on to the Egyptian desert, arriving in 383.[4]

Once in Egypt, Evagrius produced the bulk of his writings for which he is known today. It is here that he wrote on the eight thoughts, the focus of this chapter. He lived a truly ascetic life, punishing his body in ways that may have led to dying in his 50s in 399 or 400.[5] A. M. Casiday describes his lifestyle as follows:

> He ate only once per day. When he did eat, his diet was extremely limited. He assiduously abstained from lettuce, green vegetables, fruit, grapes and meat; he refrained from bathing and took no cooked food; eventually, he ruined his digestive tract and probably suffered from urinary tract stones. He slept no more than a third of the night, devoting the rest of his time to prayer, contemplation and study of Scripture. To keep himself awake, he was in the habit of walking in the courtyard of his cell. He scrupulously attended to his thoughts and, based on these observations, prepared a dossier of verses from Scripture to be cast in the face of attacking demons. If Evagrius fell victim to such an attack, he would mortify himself by undertaking spectacular measures to expose his body to the ravages of nature. This remarkable lack of self-regard took its toll and in due course Evagrius was firmly instructed by his elders in Kellia to moderate his habits.[6]

Despite the rigor of his ascetic life, many know of Evagrius principally because of something that happened over 150 years after his death. His cosmology is the part of his work for which he was most criticized.

---

3. Bamberger in Evagrius, *Praktikos*, xxxv–xxxvi.

4. Sinkewicz in Evagrius, *Evagrius of Pontus*, xvii–xviii.

5. Casiday, *Evagrius Ponticus*, 11.

6. Ibid., 13.

According to Antoine Guillaumont, his view of Christology was deemed heretical and "condemned in the *15 Anathemas Against Origen* published by Justinian in 553."[7] Guillaumont also alleges that this "Origenist Christology" states that Evagrius holds that "Jesus Christ is not truly the incarnation of the *logos*, . . . he is, rather, the enfleshed 'Christ-*nous*' . . ."[8] This is quite relevant to an overall understanding of Evagrius' work, as one must understand how Evagrius viewed heaven, hell, and higher beings.[9] Luke Dysinger writes, "According to Evagrius every order of intelligence above the human level is entrusted with responsibility for mediating divine providence. Angels . . . for human beings; archangels . . . for angels," eventually leading to Christ at the top.[10] Providence is defined as "God's ongoing provision of what each *logikos* requires in order for it to return to divine union." It is geared toward eschatological fulfillment, but is "also present in everyday experience . . ."[11] This is relevant because it describes Evagrius' worldview as centering on attaining knowledge. He follows Origen in defining heaven as a place of learning, in contrast to hell, which is a place of punishment.[12]

Elizabeth Clark, discussing the work of Antoine Guillaumont on the *Kephalaia gnostica*, states that "Evagrius's Christology was 'absolutely identical' with that of the Isochrists (who believed that in the *apokatastasis* all believers would be one with Christ) and was the decisive aspect of Origenism singled out for condemnation in the anathemas of 553."[13] There is more recent thought questioning how much of an Origenist he actually was, for example in the work of Daniël Hombergen, who is but one representative of a resurgence of Evagrian research that has come to paint him in a more positive light than previously.[14] Whether or not

7. Dysinger, *Psalmody and Prayer*, 156. His discussion on cosmology begins here.

8. Ibid.,157.

9. Ibid., 185, 194.

10. Ibid., 185.

11. Ibid., 184. A *logikos* is a reasonable being. "According to Evagrius, these were God's first, original creation, before a pre-cosmic fall into bodies. These beings were pure intellects (*noes*)." Harmless, *Desert Christians*, 368; see 368–69 for a helpful glossary of words used in Evagrian spirituality.

12. Dysinger, *Psalmody and Prayer*, 194.

13. Clark, *Origenist Controversy*, 249.

14. Casiday, "Gabriel Bunge," 269–71. These pages discuss Hombergen's contribution, but the whole of the article discusses the various schools of thought on Evagrius.

Evagrius was a follower of Origen's teachings is not overly pertinent to this study, at least in regard to his orthodoxy, because the focus is on his discussion of thoughts, demons, and prayer. However, this question is an important part of Evagrian scholarship and is related at least in part to a discussion on the dominant Western tradition regarding evil.

In sum, there are three points relevant to this study to be gained by looking at Evagrius' life in relation to his writings. First, it is noteworthy that he studied with and was close to the Cappadocian Fathers, as this lays the groundwork for his later writings. His abilities as a theologian should be evident from this early background. Although his writings are more practical and spiritual in nature, they proceed from this theological bedrock. Casiday states that Evagrius "maintained an outspoken apologetic for Nicene orthodoxy," during his time in the desert.[15] Hence, his spiritual exploration is undergirded by a care for orthodox theology. When reading Evagrius, it is important to keep in mind this theological foundation. Second, the reason he left Asia Minor and moved to Jerusalem is also important to his ascetic writings. The moral battles he fought in the desert must have been influenced by the moral battle he lived out in his life's journey. Third, the life he lived in Egypt was a battle physically, emotionally, and spiritually. As previously noted, he punished his body in extreme ways. In addition, he was never truly received by his peers, as many saw him as an outsider due to his Greek Byzantine connections.[16] Notably, the spiritual battle he fought in his own mind may also be intimately linked to his own physical and emotional battles. In this way, a fuller picture of his life helps to shed a bit of light on this internal battle.

2. *Introduction to the Eight Thoughts*

The focus of this particular study is on Evagrius' discussion of the eight thoughts, which describe the internal battle of the Christian (in his case monk) with the external demonic forces. The eight thoughts are important historically to the West because they were later edited down by Gregory the Great into the seven deadly sins. Evagrius' thoughts were transmitted to the West through Cassian, where Gregory was able to engage them.[17]

15. Casiday, *Evagrius Ponticus*, 12.

16. Bamberger in Evagrius, *Praktikos*, xlv.

17. Stewart, *Cassian the Monk*, 179n23. Also mentioned in McGinn, "Asceticism and the Emergence of the Monastic Tradition," 68–70.

As previously noted the eight thoughts are: gluttony, fornication, avarice, sadness, anger, acedia, vainglory, and pride.[18] The next section will discuss the thoughts in more depth, but it is important to see that they are part of a larger spiritual cosmology.

Evagrius sees the spiritual journey of the monk happening in stages, starting with the practices, moving toward contemplation of natural things, then immaterial things, and eventually reaching the ultimate goal of knowledge of the Trinity.[19] The goal of the monk is to achieve this knowledge in a state of "pure prayer," an imageless form of prayer, also known as the "place of God," where a monk sees a sapphire-blue light.[20] The thoughts are external, demonic attacks that hinder the monk in his quest to achieve these higher states of contemplation. An important distinction should be made related to the thoughts: Evagrius describes both *logismos* or "thought," and *noēma*, which is a "'concept' or 'depiction.'" The *logismos* is external, and the *noēma* is internal. Columba Stewart describes a sub-differentiation: the *noēma* and the *noēmata*. He states, "Sometimes *logismos* can describe input from angelic or purely human sources (*Thoughts* 8, 31). The word emphasizes origination, while *noēma* emphasizes operation: *noēmata* are simply the way the mind functions, they are its currency."[21] He goes on to state that Evagrius holds the same view as Aristotle, with the mind "creating an inner world of conceptual depictions relating to the things external to the self." Thus Evagrius differentiates between external and internal thought, but he is not always consistent, showing the difficulty of making this distinction.[22] This chapter focuses on the thoughts predominately, although a further study of *noēmata* may be helpful later in a discussion on evil and cognitive science. The thoughts are key to Evagrian writings and his worldview, and will be dealt with individually to expound the specifics of each thought.

Before moving onward, there are three terms that should be defined: passion, *apatheia*, and impassibility. Understanding the way they are used is helpful for understanding the work of Evagrius. First, he defines passion as "most generally, that which produces psychic disturbance and dis-

18. Sinkewicz in Evagrius, *Evagrius of Pontus*, xxvi.

19. Stewart, "Imageless Prayer," 178.

20. Bamberger in Evagrius, *Praktikos*, xc–xci. Also see Stewart, "Imageless Prayer," 195.

21. Stewart, "Imageless Prayer," 186–87, quotations from 187.

22. Ibid., 187.

traction, scattering creative energies and dissipating joy."[23] The passions will be revisited many times in this chapter as well as the next. Second, *apatheia* is freedom from the passions. It is the state of mind one reaches when thoughts do not bother any longer.[24] *Apatheia* is discussed further in the third-chapter presentation of the work of Pierre Hadot. Third, impassibility is connected to *apatheia*, in that it is the stage at which the monk "experiences no passion with respect to objects" *and* "remains untroubled even with regard to the memories of them."[25] Impassibility is an advanced stage in the life of the monk's progress. It will be apparent how this fits in with Evagrius' study of the thoughts as we move forward.

How the Eight Thoughts Are Germane to a Discussion on Evil

The thoughts are germane to a discussion of evil in a broader sense, but Evagrius' work is specifically important on a few different levels. First, it gives a historical, monastic viewpoint of how evil is experienced in the mind of the monk, specifically from Evagrius' perspective. Second, it gives a practical, spiritual way to engage (i.e., defeat) this evil. Third, it opens a door to explain how the mind experiences evil using supernatural language that may be interpreted to open dialogue with modern cognitive science. An example of this language is found in Evagrius' work *To Eulogios. On the Confession of Thoughts and Counsel in their Regard*, where he states:

> The demons make war on the soul by means of thoughts and they are countered in turn with a more difficult warfare by means of perseverance; and in fear they then go to battle, regarding with suspicion the mighty commander of the match. If you wish to lead your army against the phalanx of the demons, bar the gates of your soul with stillness, listen acutely to the words of your spiritual father in order that you may then set fire to the thorns of the passions even more than those of the thoughts.[26]

23. Burrus, "Praying Is Joying," 195–196.

24. Wilken, *Remembering the Christian Past*, 150.

25. *Praktikos* 67 (*Evagrius of Pontus*, 109).

26. *To Eulogios* 15 (ibid., 42). The first chapter presented this quotation in part, but the full paragraph is helpful here.

Without offering a full exegesis, the text portrays a spiritual warfare over the soul of the monk. The militaristic language presents a metaphor that gives the reader a sense of the spiritual battle within oneself, which must be overcome by persevering. This metaphorical language is of use in describing the struggle against moral evil in Evagrius' day as well as today.

The Eight Thoughts

The eight thoughts listed above are referenced in more than one of his works, but especially in the *Praktikos*, *On the Eight Thoughts* (*OET*), and *On Thoughts* (*OT*).[27] For Evagrius, there are three types of thoughts: human, angelic, and demonic. Using the element gold as an example in discussing these three thoughts, he states, "angelic thoughts are concerned with the investigation of the natures of things and search out their spiritual principles. . . . The demonic thought neither knows nor understands these things," but focuses on the "enjoyment and esteem" that comes from the acquisition of things (in this case gold). A human thought is not interested in the acquisition of the thing, but "merely introduces in the intellect the simple form of gold," or whatever one uses as an example.[28] Basically, angelic thoughts try to understand things, demonic thoughts focus on the perversion of the thing, and human thoughts focus on introducing the thing itself to the mind. For a study on evil, the demonic thoughts are of most import, but must be seen in conjunction with the other two types. It is also noteworthy that Robert Sinkewicz points out that Evagrius divides demons into two groups, one that tempts the "human (rational) part of our nature and those that act upon the animal (irrational-instinctive) part." The human part deals more with the vices that affect the rational will, for example, vainglory, pride, and envy.[29] This distinction may be helpful in conceptualizing the fourth-century view of the human person as comprised of two aspects or natures.

27. Found in ibid. beginning on pages 73, 95, and 153, respectively.

28. *On Thoughts* 8 (ibid., 158). In most cases I have tried to follow Sinkewicz's notation for marking Evagrius' work.

29. Sinkewicz, introduction to *On Thoughts* (ibid., 139).

Gluttony

Gluttony, along with avarice and vainglory, are referred to as fundamental thoughts, "those ranged first in battle." This is noteworthy, as Evagrius goes on to state that "it is not possible to fall into the hands of the spirit of fornication, unless one has fallen under the influence of gluttony."[30] Along these lines, Evagrius mentions that too much moisture in the diet gives rise to other passions, such as sexual desire.[31] He states in *OET*, "Vigilant thinking is found in the driest regimen; a life of moist diet plunges the mind into the deep."[32] In this vein, Evagrius' medical knowledge told him that avoiding a moist diet would lessen semen production and therefore limit sexual desire.[33] Evagrius calls gluttony "the mother of fornication."[34]

For the monk, gluttony is not the temptation to gorge himself to excess, but rather anxiety over the body's well-being and the boredom associated "with an unvaried diet."[35] Therefore, at least for the monk, gluttony was not necessarily thought of in the same manner as today. In *OT* Evagrius states, "When the demon of gluttony is powerless to corrupt the self-control that has been imprinted . . . he casts the mind into a desire for stricter asceticism." He goes on later to state that it is good for the monk to eat oil, bread, and water, assuming that one is not eating to satiety.[36] Again, this shows that the demon of gluttony is not only the temptation to eat too much food, but can also be manifest in the misuse of food by total deprivation.

Moving to Evagrius' structure of the knowledge of God (the path of increasing knowledge through the practices and culminating with the "place of God"), he states, again in *OET*, "A soiled mirror does not produce a clear image of the form that falls upon it; when the intellect is blunted by satiety, it does not receive the knowledge of God."[37] If one cannot get past the initial problem with gluttony, one will not know the place of God. For Evagrius, the fight against gluttony is the first part of the journey in

---

30. *On Thoughts* 1 (ibid., 153).
31. Sinkewicz, introduction to *On the Eight Thoughts* (ibid., 68).
32. *On the Eight Thoughts* 1.13 (ibid., 74).
33. Sinkewicz, introduction to *On the Eight Thoughts* (ibid., 68).
34. *On the Vices Opposed to the Virtues* 1.2 (Evagrius, *Evagrius of Pontus*, 62).
35. Sinkewicz's introduction (ibid., xxvi).
36. *On Thoughts* 35 (Casiday, *Evagrius Ponticus*, 112).
37. *On the Eight Thoughts* 1.17 (Evagrius, *Evagrius of Pontus*, 74).

one's practical life. Too much food creates laziness and a dulling of the mind, thus preventing one from knowing God.[38] Ultimately this is what the monk is trying to attain, and thus overcoming gluttony is a key part of this journey. As he does with all subsequent thoughts in *On the Vices Opposed to the Virtues* (OVOV), Evagrius pairs abstinence as the counter to gluttony.[39]

Fornication

Fornication comes after gluttony in Evagrius' listing of the eight thoughts. As the discussion of gluttony has shown, fornication follows on the failure to defeat the demon of gluttony. In *OET*, Evagrius references satiety more than once as a cause of fornication, stating that it is a "licentious impulse that is fired by satiety."[40] His discussion of fornication in this work focuses on avoidance of women in order not to stir up this passion. Many times he refers to avoidance of "encounters with women" and even refers to seeing a woman as "a poisoned arrow."[41] He explicitly states that the very "sight of a woman arouses the licentious person to pleasure . . ."[42]

Fornication refers to sexual temptation in both thought and deed. Evagrius prescribes avoiding satiety, avoiding women, and practicing control over one's thoughts.[43] He states in the *Praktikos*:

> The demon of fornication compels one to desire various bodies. It attacks more violently those who practise abstinence in order that they give it up, convinced that they are accomplishing nothing. In defiling the soul, the demon inclines it to shameful deeds, has it speak and hear certain things, almost as if the object were visible and present.[44]

This presents the two-pronged attack of this demon, in that it compels the mind to action or thought. The monk is affected as if the object were present. It bears mentioning that this visible object brought on by the demon

38. Sinkewicz, introduction to *On the Eight Thoughts* (ibid., 68).

39. *On the Vices Opposed to the Virtues* 1(2) (ibid., 62).

40. *On the Eight Thoughts* 2.11 (ibid., 77). Satiety is also mentioned in 2.12.

41. *On the Eight Thoughts* 2.2, 2.8, 2.10 (ibid., 76–77), as well as many other mentions of "encounters with women." "A poisoned arrow" is from 2.6.

42. *On the Eight Thoughts* 2.17 (ibid., 77).

43. Sinkewicz, introduction to *On the Eight Thoughts* (ibid., 69).

44. *Praktikos* 8 (ibid., 98).

would be a hindrance to the "imageless" prayer that Evagrius is ultimately trying to achieve. It also is an example of why images may cause sin, and hence why one should strive for pure prayer devoid of images.

In multiple admonishments in *OET*, Evagrius tells the reader to avoid spending too much time thinking about women.[45] The mind's thoughts are tied closely to sin, and not only possible action. Again, as is similar with gluttony, it attacks the one who abstains more than one who does not. Also of note is the language used in the *Praktikos*, referring to the "soul" of the monk. Use of terms must be noted in dealing in the historical monastic worldview, as well as with modern conceptions of the world in the cognitive sciences, as they sometimes have different meanings.[46]

It is notable that Evagrius focuses on the intellect and thinking in regard to fornication. This is further brought out in *To Eulogios*, where he uses language of warfare and speaks of demons dislodging "one's thinking with shameful pleasures." He states, "Sometimes the thoughts attract the passions and sometimes the passions the thoughts," but both are used in making war on the soul.[47] The use of passions is important and here Evagrius is drawing on the Ancient Greek tradition. This is explained further in the next chapter in the discussion of Pierre Hadot's work.

Although, Evagrius is very harsh toward women in this section, the admonitions are clear: women will draw you in and cause you to fall.[48] It is worth mentioning that perhaps Evagrius is drawing on his own encounter with a married woman and the struggle it caused him. The fervor he expresses in this section may indicate that it is of particular import to him, especially as this is one thought that can passionately, and particularly, be incited by another person. Evagrius pairs fornication with the virtue of chastity.[49]

Avarice

The third thought of the eight is that of avarice (or greed). Evagrius notes, quoting Paul in 1 Timothy 6:10, that "'Avarice is the root of all evils.'" He

45. *On the Eight Thoughts*, examples in 2.19 and 2.20 (ibid., 76–78).

46. Thanks to Robert A. Cathey for mentioning this in discussions on this project. This was addressed in more detail in the introductory chapter to this book.

47. *To Eulogios* 13 (*Evagrius of Pontus*, 39).

48. This is found repeatedly in the section on fornication in *On the Eight Thoughts* (ibid., 76–77). See note 41 above, referencing "encounters with women."

49. *On the Vices Opposed to the Virtues* 2(2) (ibid., 62–63).

also gives great warning about this thought, stating, "the demon of avarice is the most varied and ingenious in deceit." As many other thoughts are connected to each other, Evagrius connects avarice with the demons of vainglory and pride.[50]

Avarice is defined as an "attachment to possessions" and "ties to material realities." In addition, "Possessions are treated as burdens that can only cause anxieties and worries, and in their absence one succumbs to a sense of loss and frustration that Evagrius calls sadness." He even defines avarice to include the memory of things the monk might hold on to, hence becoming a burden, because it shows that the monk has not fully renounced the world.[51] Therefore, it is not only the present ownership of a thing itself, but even one-time ownership. A simpler way of putting it would be to say that a person cannot miss something that they never had, and that once they leave goods behind, they must also forget about them.

In *OET* Evagrius uses similes, depicting an unencumbered monk who is like "a high-soaring eagle," "an athlete who cannot be thrown," and "a light runner who speedily attains 'the prize'" (in reference to Philippians 3:14).[52] He also employs metaphor in stating that the monk is "a well-prepared traveler" and "light on the wings, not weighed down by concerns."[53] In contrast, the one who succumbs to avarice "has bound himself with the fetters of his worries, as a dog is tied to a leash."[54]

The discussion of avarice ends with an interesting contrast that enforces Evagrius' pathway for the monk as one of leaving the physical for the spiritual. He alludes to Matthew 6:20 in contrasting a greedy person who collects gold with one who "'lays up treasure in heaven'" and discusses the person who "'makes an image and puts it in hiding' (Deuteronomy 27:15)."[55] The emphasis again is on the spiritual treasure, a biblical theme, for sure, but also a reiteration of the path a monk must take to attain the "place" of the Trinity.

---

50. *On Thoughts* 21 (ibid., 167–68; also in Casiday, *Evagrius Ponticus*, 103–4).

51. Sinkewicz, introduction to *On the Eight Thoughts* (Evagrius, *Evagrius of Pontus*, 70).

52. *On the Eight Thoughts* 3.5, 3.10 (ibid., 78–79).

53. *On the Eight Thoughts* 3.4, 3.6 (ibid., 78).

54. *On the Eight Thoughts* 3.7 (ibid., 79).

55. *On the Eight Thoughts* 3.13, 3.14 (ibid.).

In *OVOV*, Evagrius pairs avarice with "freedom from possessions," which leads to more freedoms.[56] Avarice is key among the *logismoi* because it represents a contrast between material possession and spiritual freedom. It epitomizes the journey a monk must take to be free of this world's encumbrances.

Anger

Next among the thoughts is anger.[57] Anger is the "most virulent allergen in the monastic life."[58] It "is the dominant characteristic of the demonic. The person consumed by anger gradually loses his humanity . . ." leading to "madness and a loss of one's wits, manifested in hallucinations and terrifying nightmares."[59]

Anger is clearly one of the most important thoughts for Evagrius. This is borne out in his description of the way it irritates the monk and makes a person unstable, in contrast to one who is peaceful. He describes an angry person as a "wild boar" and says that anger "makes the soul wild." He goes on to contrast the angry person as a lion who "rattles the hinges" of his cage with "a state of peace" like dolphins diving in a calm sea.[60] His description of anger also references irritation, which is the opposite of the monk's strivings in opening himself up to God. This is shown in his emphasis on prayer. Anger is most deadly when the monk goes to pray. He compares the irritation of smoke in a person's eyes to that of anger irritating the mind in prayer.[61] He writes in the *Praktikos* that it "seizes the mind" and can turn into resentment and even "attacks of venomous wild beasts."[62] The manner in which anger is described is wild and animal-like

---

56. *On the Vices Opposed to the Virtue* 3(3) (ibid., 63).

57. In the *Praktikos* and *On the Vices Opposed to the Virtues* sadness comes before anger. The orders can be found in Evagrius, *Evagrius of Pontus*, 98–99 and 63–64, respectively. However, in *On the Eight Thoughts* sadness follows anger. Sinkewicz discusses this in his introduction to *On the Eight Thoughts* (ibid., 71). I am choosing to follow this latter order, as the way Evagrius describes sadness as "constituted from thoughts of anger" lends itself better to this ordering. *On the Eight Thoughts* 5.1 (ibid., 81).

58. Stewart, "Evagrius Ponticus," 66.

59. Sinkewicz, introduction to *On the Eight Thoughts* (Evagrius, *Evagrius of Pontus*, 71).

60. *On the Eight Thoughts* 4.4, 4.1, 4.7, 4.8, respectively for the quotations (ibid., 80).

61. *On the Eight Thoughts* 4.16 (ibid., 81).

62. *Praktikos* 5.11 (ibid., 99). Evagrius also mentions that "an angry person imagines attacks of wild beasts" in *On the Eight Thoughts* 4.20 (ibid., 81).

as these examples show. It runs contrary to the monk's wish for control and discipline and keeps the mind from focus.

As in this contrast of wildness and peace, Evagrius presents another major example of how a demon keeps a person from attaining the state of pure prayer. He writes, "the movement of irascibility thickens the intellect of the angry person" and "the irascible person is troubled by senseless thoughts," while "a soul without anger becomes a temple of the Holy Spirit" and "an intellect at peace becomes a shelter for the Holy Trinity."[63] The angry person cannot attain to pure prayer. Anger is a great adversary for the mind in the struggle for peace. While one is affected by anger, one cannot pray properly.

The counterpart of anger is patience.[64] In *OET*, the patient person is described as one who, "free from resentment discourses on spiritual matters and receives in the night the answers to mysteries."[65] Again, anger clouds the ability to see spiritual truth, and patience will bring knowledge. This description still bears fruit in a modern context, as anger can cloud a person's judgment.

Sadness

Following anger is sadness. Sadness "is constituted from thoughts of anger, for irascibility is a longing for revenge, and the frustration of revenge produces sadness."[66] It seems to follow a basic flow of thought. When anger does not satisfy a person, that frustration leads to sadness. Sadness bogs down the monk in a seeming state of apathy, in which the monk as "a prisoner of the passions is bound with sadness."[67]

In the *Praktikos* Evagrius describes sadness as entering "through the frustration of one's desires" or following from anger. If it occurs through the former, it is because the monk remembers his former life, realizing that the pleasures from that life can no longer be had.[68] In this way, sadness is a type of "depression" brought on by wishing things were different than they are. From this it is possible to see how the "sadness" of

---

63. *On the Eight Thoughts* 4.5, 4.3, 4.11, 4.12, respectively (ibid., 80).

64. *On the Vices Opposed to the Virtues* 4(3) (ibid., 64).

65. *On the Eight Thoughts*, 4.21 (ibid., 81).

66. *On the Eight Thoughts*, 5.1 (ibid.).

67. *On the Eight Thoughts* 5.8 (ibid., 82).

68. *Praktikos* 4.10 (ibid., 98).

Evagrius became "envy" in the seven deadly sins of Gregory the Great: it stems from wishing one had something one does not. The difference in Evagrius, it would seem, is that this reminiscing brings about something more like a depressed feeling, versus other feelings that may be associated with envy. Envy also refers to the desire of the goods or life belonging to others, while sadness seems to refer to the desire of things that the monk himself had at one time. Envy could be seen to lead to anger, and likewise, sadness is closely linked to anger.[69]

The symbol of sadness is the viper, which Evagrius describes as containing a nature that is "beneficial to humans" because it can destroy the venom of other creatures, but when uncontrolled "it destroys the living creature itself."[70] There is a clear indication here that sadness can be used in a positive way for the soul. In *OET* he states, "A smelting-furnace purifies base silver; a godly sadness (cf. 2 Cor. 7:10) purifies a soul caught in sins."[71] Also interesting is that as sadness and anger are switched in the order of the thoughts, depending on which Evagrian work one references (see note 57 in this chapter), in *OET*, where anger comes first, Evagrius refers to thoughts of anger as "a viper's offspring."[72] This lends some credence to the idea that anger comes from sadness, but also that sadness can come from anger, as stated earlier.

Even more so than the previous thoughts, Evagrius describes sadness as blocking the way to pure prayer. He writes in *OET*, "A monk afflicted by sadness cannot move the mind towards contemplation or offer up pure prayer, for sadness poses an obstacle to all that is good." He goes on to state that "worldly sadness diminishes the mind," that "sadness dulls the mind's capacity for contemplation," and that "sadness takes away the perception of the soul."[73] Clearly sadness is one of the most difficult adversaries for the monk. It is fitting then, that in *OVOV* Evagrius pairs sadness with joy as its counterpart. This is because joy would indicate contentment and happiness with the state of a monk's life. Notable in this description is that joy is "a partner in patience," further connecting the thoughts of

---

69. For a brief discussion on envy see Newhauser, "Introduction," 4. He also mentions how Gregory drew on the eight thoughts of Evagrius.

70. *On Thoughts* 12 (Evagrius, *Evagrius of Pontus*, 161).

71. *On the Eight Thoughts* 5.19 (ibid., 83).

72. *On the Eight Thoughts* 4.17 (ibid., 81).

73. *On the Eight Thoughts* 5.6, 5.20, 5.21, 5.25, respectively (ibid., 82–83).

anger and sadness, being that anger's counterpart is patience. In addition, sadness is "a kinsman of acedia," the next thought in the list.[74]

Acedia

Acedia follows sadness in the thoughts. Sinkewicz describes it succinctly: "The monk afflicted with acedia will turn anywhere to avoid the task at hand."[75] Acedia is distinct from sloth, its counterpart in the seven deadly sins, because it is more a distraction than a form of laziness. Boredom or restlessness may be an appropriate way to describe it. The theme of Evagrius' writing on acedia is that of a distracted monk, who will look for anything else to do except that which is to be done. He describes it as "a relaxation of the soul," but infers that it is one that is "not in accord with nature." The person suffering from acedia is like a "waterless cloud . . . chased away by a wind," and goes on to contrast a "feeble plant" taken by a breeze with a "well-rooted tree" that is not moved by wind.[76] Such is the contrast between one affected by acedia and one who is not.

In the *Praktikos*, Evagrius cites acedia as "the most oppressive of all the demons," appropriately calling it "the noonday demon."[77] He presents a description of how this demon works that would be familiar to anyone in the present day who has worked in any kind of office employment:

> He attacks the monk about the fourth hour [viz. 10 a.m.] and be-
> sieges his soul until the eighth hour [2 p.m.]. First of all, he makes
> it appear that the sun moves slowly or not at all, and that the day
> seems to be fifty hours long. Then he compels the monk to look
> constantly towards the windows, to jump out of the cell, to watch
> the sun to see how far it is from the ninth hour [3 p.m.], to look
> this way and that lest one of the brothers . . .[78]

Clearly some things do not change over time. One can almost feel the demon overcome him while reading this description. In addition, the monk who suffers from it is never satisfied. Evagrius compares a man not satisfied with a single wife with a monk not satisfied with a single cell, and

74. *On the Vices Opposed to the Virtues* 4(3) (ibid., 63).

75. Sinkewicz, introduction to *On the Eight Thoughts* (ibid., 72).

76. *On the Eight Thoughts* 5.1, 5.3, 5.8, 5.9, respectively (ibid., 83–84).

77. *Praktikos* 6.12 (ibid., 99).

78. Ibid. Sinkewicz also notes that the ending to this passage parallels *On the Eight Thoughts* 6.14 in Evagrius, *Evagrius of Pontus*, 250n21.

compares a "sick person" not satisfied with one type of food with a monk not being satisfied "with a single type of work."[79] The monk who suffers from acedia is always looking for something else to do.

Additionally, as before, the monk's distraction from prayer and contemplation is the focus. "The monk afflicted with acedia is lazy in prayer and will not even say the words of a prayer."[80] Fittingly, the counterpart to acedia is perseverance.[81] Evagrius calls it the cure for acedia and implores his readers to set a goal and work until they reach it, and to "Pray with understanding and intensity, and the spirit of acedia will flee from you."[82] For Evagrius, overcoming acedia is a matter of mind over matter. One must battle through it by focus and action.

Vainglory

For Evagrius, vainglory is "any desire for human esteem" that interferes with "all the virtues and practices of the ascetic life."[83] In other words, vainglory deals with the human in regard to priorities of life. This will be contrasted by the last of the thoughts, pride. It is one of the fundamental thoughts, as mentioned previously in the section on gluttony.[84] Vainglory undermines the work of the monk in the ascetic practices and prayers. This is evidenced from Evagrius' descriptions of it in *OET*. He explicitly states, "vainglory destroys the rewards of the virtues" and "virtue is ruined when it leans on vainglory."[85] Implicit in his discussion of vainglory here is that the practical life of the monk is not only dependent on the work itself, but the reason for the work. Good works performed with a selfish attitude or for a faulty reason are empty and useless. He goes on to compare such "virtue" to "a flawed sacrificial victim" that "cannot be brought to the altar of God."[86] As with the other thoughts, vainglory will prevent a person from reaching the state of pure prayer, and in a manner explicit to

---

79. *On the Eight Thoughts*, 6.13, 6.12 (Evagrius, *Evagrius of Pontus*, 84).

80. *On the Eight Thoughts*, 6.16 (ibid.).

81. *On the Vices Opposed to the Virtues* 6(4) (ibid., 64).

82. *On the Eight Thoughts* 6.18 (ibid., 85).

83. Sinkewicz, the introduction to *On the Eight Thoughts* (ibid., 72).

84. *On Thoughts* 1 (ibid., 153).

85. *On the Eight Thoughts* 7.5, 7.3 (ibid., 85).

86. *On the Eight Thoughts*, 7.16 (ibid., 86).

the path. Not only does vainglory serve as a stumbling block to the monk, it erases the path of virtue itself by rendering the monk's work useless.

In addition, in *OT* Evagrius speaks of the utmost danger of vainglory, stating, "Alone among the thoughts, that of vainglory has a surfeit of material, embraces nearly the entire inhabited world and opens the doors to all the demons, like a wicked man betraying a city."[87] He later goes on to state, "All the demons, once they have been defeated, join in exaggerating the thought of vainglory, and again through it they all have an entrance into the soul . . ."[88] Clearly the ordering of the thoughts is important to note here, because it is once the other thoughts have been defeated that vainglory enters and rehabilitates them for use once again.

Furthermore, vainglory is linked to both pride and fornication. Pride is mentioned in *OT* in reference to vainglory: "From this thought is also born that of pride . . ."[89] This will be picked up in the next section. Fornication is mentioned in the section of the *Praktikos* on vainglory: "Sometimes it delivers him over to the demon of fornication, he who a little earlier was a holy priest carried off in bonds."[90] This seems notable, as mentioned in the section on fornication, because Evagrius may be referring to himself in mentioning the holy priest. Perhaps he is saying that his own vainglory led to fornication in his previous commission of adultery in Asia Minor. Lastly, it is interesting that Evagrius uses "freedom from vainglory" as the counterpart to vainglory in *OVOV*, while for most thoughts he refers to a descriptive opposite.[91]

Pride

Last among the eight thoughts is pride. Sinkewicz writes that "pride is fundamentally the failure to acknowledge God as the source of all virtue and goodness in one's life," and that God's help is needed in all ascetic accomplishments.[92] Different from vainglory, pride is failure to give God credit for good works. As mentioned in the previous section, vainglory

---

87. *On Thoughts* 14 (Casiday, *Evagrius Ponticus*, 99; also in Evagrius, *Evagrius of Pontus*, 162).

88. *On Thoughts* 14 (Casiday, *Evagrius Ponticus*, 99).

89. Ibid.

90. *Praktikos* 7.13 (Evagrius, *Evagrius of Pontus*, 100).

91. *On the Vices Opposed to the Virtues* 7(4) (ibid., 64).

92. Sinkewicz, introduction to *On the Eight Thoughts* (ibid., 72).

can open the door to pride, which is reiterated in *OET* where Evagrius states, "A flash of lightning foretells the sound of thunder; vainglory announces the presence of pride."[93]

Evagrius' description of pride is quite grotesque; the section on pride in *OET* opens with "Pride is a tumour of the soul filled with pus; when it has ripened, it will rupture and create a great disgusting mess."[94] Pride can be viewed as the worst of the thoughts in that it leaves the person guilty of it without hope, "abandoned by God and given over to the demons who then plague the poor fellow with terrifying fantasies and hallucinations until he is overcome by a kind of cowardly paranoia."[95] One must realize the danger in engaging this demon.

In looking at the amount of text devoted to each thought in *OET*, Evagrius spent the most space on pride. More than a couple of sub-chapters in this section go beyond the two-line proverbial style that is typical of this work. Chapter 8.12 in particular is quite lengthy and engages Scripture to a high degree.[96] Evagrius employs the images of the staff and the serpent quite a bit in this text, making clear allusion to the Pentateuch. There is reference to both the serpent that "bites and kills" and the bronze serpent that heals. Imagery from the Torah is plentiful in this section in particular.[97]

Furthermore, pride is coupled with humility in *OVOV*.[98] Humility is referenced more than once in *OET*. Evagrius states that "The word of a humble person is a soothing ointment for the soul" and "Humility is the parapet of a housetop" that keeps one safe.[99] Pride is clearly dangerous because it is in direct contradiction with God's order. If one is proud, he has indeed entered dangerous territory.

---

93. *On the Eight Thoughts* 8.2 (ibid., 87).

94. *On the Eight Thoughts* 8.1 (ibid.).

95. Sinkewicz, introduction to *On the Eight Thoughts* (ibid., 72).

96. *On the Eight Thoughts* (ibid., 73–90; the section on pride is found on 87–90).

97. *On the Eight Thoughts* 8.23–29 (ibid., 89); quotation from 8.27. In addition, the Passover is mentioned in 8.21, and "Laban the Syrian" is mentioned in 8.22. Sinkewicz mentions the scriptural references of Exodus 4:3–4 as well as Numbers 21:6, 9, specifically, which cover both the story of the staff becoming a snake and returning to a staff (2.25–26), and the bronze serpent in the wilderness that the Israelites could look upon and be healed when they were dying from snake bites (2.27–28).

98. *On the Vices Opposed to the Virtues* 9(4) (ibid., 65).

99. *On the Eight Thoughts* 8.18, 8.32 (ibid., 88, 90).

Additional Notes on the Thoughts

As should be apparent by now, the eight thoughts are diverse in threat and treatment and prevent a person from engaging in true knowledge of God. In this way, for Evagrius, evil is an obstacle in the attainment of truly knowing the Trinity. The thoughts or demons are one major key to the Evagrian cosmology in that they prevent the monk from attaining pure prayer. It is of note that in *OET* Evagrius only once uses the term "demon" and only four times uses "the formula 'the spirit of x.'" This is different from most of his works that engage the thoughts. He uses "demon" or "demonic" "55 times in *Eulogios*, 72 times in the *Praktikos*, and 98 times in *Thoughts*."[100] For purposes of this study, the term "thoughts" is of great use, but given the fourth-century usage of the demonic, both must be at the heart of the analysis. It is interesting that in a work dedicated solely to the eight thoughts Evagrius would avoid using other descriptive terms.

Also of note is that in *OVOV* Evagrius mentions a ninth thought, jealousy. This is the only place in Evagrius' lists of thoughts where there are nine, although he mentions jealousy elsewhere in his writings.[101] He pairs it with "freedom from jealousy" just as he pairs vainglory with "freedom from vainglory."[102] Interestingly, he links jealousy with vainglory in the *Eulogios*.[103]

Remedies for the Eight Thoughts

Now that a catalog of the thoughts has been established, it is necessary to discuss Evagrius' worldview in a more detailed manner, as well as ways in which these thoughts can be combated using Scripture and prayer.

The Thoughts and Prayer

It has already been established that there are three types of thoughts: angelic, human, and demonic. In addition, there are two classes of demons: those that tempt the rational part of a person and those that tempt the irrational. Evagrius gives examples of vainglory and pride as those that

---

100. Sinkewicz, introduction to *On the Eight Thoughts* (ibid., 73).

101. Sinkewicz, introduction to *On the Vices Opposed to the Virtues* (ibid., 61).

102. *On the Vices Opposed o the Virtues* 8 (4) and 7(4) (ibid., 65, 64, respectively).

103. Sinkewicz, introduction to *On the Vices Opposed to the Virtues* (ibid., 61).

tempt the rational self.[104] In *OT*, in addition to these observations, Evagrius goes into greater depth about the classifications of demons/thoughts and how they work than in *OET*, where he focuses on the individual types of thoughts. The following are a few important observations from *OT*.

Notably, one cannot hold two thoughts at the same time. He references chapter 17 of *OT* in chapter 24, stating "that no impure thought arises within us without a sensible object." Although he acknowledges that the mind moves between thoughts rapidly, two thoughts cannot be held at one time. Because the mind cannot hold two thoughts at once, Evagrius recommends when a demonic thought enters the mind to transfer to "another mental representation" because if the mind does not, the thought may become sinful action.[105] Evagrius presents two modes for fighting demons. First, an analysis of where the thought comes from, moving through the following list: "the mind that received the thought, the mental representation of the sensible object, the sensible object itself, and the passion that is motivating the thought." This leads to finding "the locus of sinfulness" and the exposure of the tactics used by the thought. The demon then loses its power. The second method, as previously mentioned, is "using good thoughts to dispel evil ones." This technique is only useful for those who "have already attained at least the initial stages of natural contemplation"; a certain level of monastic maturity is needed.[106] This fits into Evagrius' order of monastic discipline on the path to knowledge of the Trinity. This method suggests an active replacement, as opposed to the former, which is a pinpointing of the source of the problem where knowledge equals power.

In addition, the thoughts can affect a person through dreams. Evagrius apportions three successive chapters in *OT* to dreams. The discussion presents how dreams from the night before can sometimes cause the monk to fall into sin the next day. Dreams can affect him in different ways, whether this be in fornication, vainglory, or sadness. "Anchorites must therefore keep vigil and pray that they may not enter into temptation . . ." In contrast, angelic dreams also affect the monk in a positive manner by containing peace and joy.[107] This follows the discussion on the different

---

104. *On Thoughts* 18 (ibid., 165). The three types of thoughts were discussed earlier this chapter.

105. *On Thoughts* 24 (ibid., 169–70).

106. Sinkewicz, introduction to *On Thoughts* (ibid., 150–51).

107. *On Thoughts* 27–29 (ibid., 172–74, quotation on 172).

types of thoughts, with angelic thoughts being at the opposite end of the spectrum from demonic ones. Evagrius even links sleep with images and a person's health. He states, "When the natural movements of the body during sleep are free of images, they reveal that the soul is healthy to a certain extent. The formation of images is an indication of ill health."[108]

Prayer is important for the monk because it is only through the power of God that the monk can defeat the thoughts. In the short treatise *A Word about Prayer*, Evagrius states, "For you cannot be victorious by yourself, since the fight against evil thoughts is too difficult for you alone. Therefore it is essential for us to invoke God and persevere in prayer, seeing that it is he alone who is able to calm our mind."[109]

Moreover, the battle against the thoughts continues even for the monk who has attained advanced levels of prayer. In the following passage from *Chapters on Prayer*, which was alluded to in the introductory chapter, Evagrius states:

> 72. When the mind finally achieves the practice of pure prayer free from the passions, then the demons no longer attack it on the left, but on the right. They suggest to it a notion of God along with some form associated with the senses so that it thinks that it has perfectly attained the goal of prayer. A man experienced in the gnostic life said that this happens under the influence of the passion of vainglory and that of the demon who touches a place in the brain and causes palpitations in the blood vessels.

> 73. I think that the demon, by touching the spot just mentioned, alters the light around the mind as he wishes, and in this way the passion of vainglory is moved towards a thought that forms the mind heedlessly towards localizing the divine and essential knowledge. Since the mind is not troubled by the impure passions of the flesh but apparently has a pure disposition, it thinks that there is no longer any contrary activity within it, and so it supposes to be divine the manifestation that arises within it under the influence of the demon, who employs great cunning in altering through the brain the light associated with it and giving the mind a form, as we said previously.[110]

108. *Praktikos* 55 (ibid., 107).
109. Evagrius *A Word about Prayer* 3 (Casiday, *Evagrius Ponticus*, 119).
110. Evagrius *Chapters on Prayer* 72–73 (Evagrius, *Evagrius of Pontus*, 200–201).

This makes clear that for Evagrius there is an interaction between prayer, the pious mind, the demonic, and the brain. This will be an important reference in the final chapter of this work, as the text opens the door to a major interaction of language and worldview with current-day cognitive science. This is one of the few places in Evagrius that explicitly brings out language that is used in cognitive science, although this language is implicit all throughout his work.

Prayer, Scripture, and the Disciplines

Moving forward, it is helpful to take a more specific look at how prayer and discipline are used to combat the demons/thoughts within the overall cosmology of Evagrius. The corresponding virtue for each vice has been presented in the previous section. In addition, in the *Praktikos* he addresses how to defeat each of the eight thoughts.

Gluttony can be countered by limiting oneself to a smaller ration of bread and water. When one is satiated, one craves more types of food, thus encouraging gluttony. Fornication can be controlled by limiting one's use of water. This has been alluded to previously. Avarice can be defeated by charity because it is "impossible for charity to exist alongside riches in a given individual." Sadness can be stopped by fleeing worldly pleasure. He describes the person that flees this pleasure as a citadel.[111]

Evagrius devotes a large amount of space to the final four thoughts, especially anger. He presents seven chapters addressing its defeat. One theme is strength of mind, or not listening to the thoughts. He states, "Do not give yourself to the thought of anger, fighting in your intellect with the person who hurt you, nor to the thought of fornication by continually imagining the pleasure. The first brings darkness to the soul . . . both leave your mind defiled." He also suggests compassion and gentleness, as well as gift giving, as in the case of Jacob and Esau. For the monks, however, this means being hospitable because they are poor and cannot afford to give gifts.[112]

Next, he presents three chapters on remedies for acedia. As in *OVOV*, Evagrius recommends perseverance. Interestingly, in this discussion he also recommends dividing the soul into two parts, one to offer consolation and one to receive it, while doing this "with tears." He quotes Psalm

111. *Praktikos* 16–19 (ibid., 100–101, quotation on 101).
112. *Praktikos* 20–26, quotation from 23 (ibid., 101–2).

42:5–6 in this section, where the psalmist presents a contrast between a sad soul and hope in God.[113] Evagrius also mentions tears as a remedy in other works, including his *Exhortation to a Virgin*.[114]

In chapters 30–31 of the *Praktikos*, Evagrius discusses the remedy for vainglory, which is to "work devotedly at the practical life," until one attains knowledge. Once knowledge (of God) is attained, vainglory holds no sway, because the pleasures presented by vainglory pale in comparison to the knowledge attained.[115] This also shows that once the monk attains the state of pure prayer, the demons will have more difficulty because the monk has now tasted the fullness of knowledge.

Lastly, chapter 33 of *Praktikos* addresses pride. Evagrius tells the reader that pride can be remedied by remembering the past life of the monk and how he "made the transition to impassibility by the mercy of Christ." This instills humility and stops the thought of pride from entering and gaining a foothold.[116]

As these eight brief descriptions show, the *Praktikos* offers ways in which to combat the thoughts. In addition, through various writings Evagrius presents many other ways that prayer and the disciplines can be used to combat these demons.

Evagrius' work *On Prayer* is obviously key to his opinions on uses of prayer. It is in this work that the classic phrase "If you are a theologian, you will pray truly, and if you pray truly, you will be a theologian" is located.[117] He also states that "Prayer is activity that befits the dignity of the mind, that is, its best and uncontaminated activity and use."[118] For

113. *Praktikos* 27–29, specifically 27, 28 (ibid., 102–3). Sinkewicz notes the reference as Psalm 41:6, which may refer to the Septuagint, but even in this case an error is seemingly present as the Septuagint reference should be Psalm 41:5–6a. See Brenton, *Septuagint*, 722.

114. See the note in Evagrius, *Evagrius of Pontus*, 252n36. Example found in *Exhortation to a Virgin* 39 (ibid., 134).

115. *Praktikos* 30–32, quotation in 32 (ibid., 103).

116. *Praktikos* 33 (ibid.).

117. *On Prayer* 61 (Casiday, *Evagrius Ponticus*, 192); but *On Prayer* 60 in Evagrius, *Evagrius of Pontus*, 199. The difference in chapter here raises the point that there are many interesting side notes regarding textual tradition, translation, and other matters that I have chosen to leave out of this study for the sake of space and complexity. Casiday's and Sinkewicz's texts are sufficient for the theological engagement needed here. Further study in the textual tradition will only add to the richness in understanding Evagrius.

118. *On Prayer* 84 (Casiday, *Evagrius Ponticus*, 195); also *On Prayer* 84 in Evagrius, *Evagrius of Pontus*, 202.

Evagrius, prayer is at the heart of theology and at the heart of the human being. The mind's best function is to pray. This taps into a dualistic thread in Evagrius' presentation. This is clear in Columba Stewart's article "Imageless Prayer and the Theological Vision of Evagrius Ponticus." For Evagrius, the mind is most fully linked to God in prayer and when it has left the material world, thus avoiding "form or shape, since God has neither." Evagrius cautions "against mistaking sensory phenomena for experiences of God." For him, "God is above all perception (αἴσθησις) and thought (ἔννοια)."[119] The whole cosmology of Evagrian thought lends itself to a separation from material things to spiritual in the mode of prayer. In *On Prayer* he states, "You cannot practise pure prayer while entangled in material things (cf. 2 Tim. 2:4) and agitated by continuous concerns, for prayer is the laying aside of mental representations."[120] More than just communication with God, prayer is actually described here as an action to remove mental associations from the material.

As far as practical advice on prayer, Evagrius gives us many helpful quotes regarding its uses. Although much of the study thus far has been dedicated to the thoughts and their specific nature, general uses of prayer are the key component in this journey. In many ways, moral evil and the thoughts are just the foil to the attainment of pure prayer, but I do not wish to minimize their reality or substance. He describes "[o]ne who cultivates pure prayer" as one who "will hear noises, crashings, voices, and tormenting screams that come from the demons . . . . In times of temptations such as these, use a short and intense prayer."[121] Prayer is used in different ways for different occasions. His language is sometimes that of warfare: "Like an experienced fighter, be prepared to avoid being shaken with confusion . . . even if you see a sword drawn against you or a light rushing at your eyes; should you see some unsightly and bloody figure . . . take your stand, making the good confession . . ."[122] He even refers to a "saint" whom the demons attacked for two weeks, using "him as a ball, tossing him into the air and catching him on his mat. But they were not able even for a little while to bring his mind down out of his fiery prayer."[123] Prayer is not just a placid, civil event for Evagrius, but a mental

119. Stewart, "Imageless Prayer," 191.
120. *On Prayer* 70 (Evagrius, *Evagrius of Pontus*, 200).
121. *On Prayer* 97–98 (ibid., 203).
122. *On Prayer* 92 (ibid.).
123. *On Prayer* 111 (ibid., 205).

(and often physical) battle against evil. He states, "All the warfare that is waged between us and the impure demons concerns nothing other than spiritual prayer, for this is extremely offensive and odious to them, but salvific and very pleasant for us."[124]

In contrast to this, prayer is also the place of peace and the mind's best use. "Undistracted prayer is the highest function of the mind." "Prayer is the mind's ascent to God."[125] In prayer, the mind is working the best it can, which may also be why, for Evagrius, it is such a powerful tool against evil. Prayer is also a purification process for the monk: "The angel of the church of Thmuis, Serapion, said, 'The mind is perfectly purified when it has drunk spiritual knowledge; love heals the enflamed part of the *thumos* . . . and abstinence (*enkrateia*) stops the flow of evil desire."[126] This idea of purification and healing is notable, and may be useful as this study moves forward in integrating Evagrius' work with the work of others.

Although there are countless other admonitions and teachings of Evagrius on prayer, it is best to stop at this point and move forward. Evagrius uses prayer as many different tools and weapons, as well as a state of higher consciousness. For him, the mind is working best when it is at prayer.

As one moves away from prayer to a discussion of Scripture, one sees Evagrius' emphasis on the Psalms.[127] In addition, Evagrius used medical language and ideas from Greek philosophy. He draws on the Platonic tradition of psalms helping to benefit one's temperament. Plato held that "The true purpose of music does not lie in its common use to 'provoke irrational pleasure', but rather in its power to restore order and harmony in the soul afflicted with disharmony (ἀνάρμοστον)."[128] Evagrius is drawing on "an ancient philosophical and medical tradition which had become

---

124. *On Prayer* 49 (ibid., 197–98).

125. *On Prayer* 35, 36 (Casiday, *Evagrius Ponticus*, 190); but *On Prayer* 34a, 35 in Evagrius, *Evagrius of Pontus*, 196. Casiday notes in 235n16 that in some versions ch. 35 is not present and in some it is attached to ch. 34. This is the case in Sinkewicz's text.

126. Evagrius *Gnostikos* 47 (Stewart, "Evagrius Ponticus," 71).

127. The work of Luke Dysinger is especially relevant in discussing the Psalms in Evagrius. In his book *Psalmody and Prayer in the Writings of Evagrius Ponticus*, Dysinger presents the importance of Scripture, specifically Psalms, to Evagrius' work. Chapters 4–6 in Dysinger ("Psalmody as Spiritual Remedy," "The Psalter as Spiritual Weapon," and "The Psalter as Contemplative Vision") specifically deal with some of the themes already laid out in this chapter.

128. Dysinger, *Psalmody and Prayer*, 128.

almost commonplace among Christian theologians."[129] He is shown to draw on medical language as the Cappadocian Fathers did, but to a greater degree.[130] He is following Galen's suggestion that "the best physician should make use of both theoretical and empirical knowledge in treating illness." Evagrius gives weight to empirical observation, an important point to note as this study moves forward into dialogue with the cognitive sciences.[131] Of special note in this chapter is a reference to Evagrius' writing the *Thirty-three Chapters*, where he lists sixteen health problems that are found in the Bible, most from the Pentateuch, and associates these physical issues with spiritual vices. This is "uncommon among other Christian spiritual authors" and lends more credence to the connections Evagrius himself makes between the physical and the spiritual.[132] It is notable that Evagrius links many if not most of these maladies with the rational part of a human being. "Sicknesses" from gonorrhea to stuttering are linked to the rational soul.[133]

Dysinger also presents the importance of spiritual warfare for Evagrius and how psalms are at the fore of the way of life for the monk. Psalms are used "as both a textbook and a spiritual arsenal for the *praktikos*, as well as a source of allegories on which the *gnostikos* should meditate." He then goes on to state that psalms are important for spiritual warfare in the *Antirrhetikos*.[134] Chapter 5 of Dysinger's work is also of special interest to this study, in part because he there presents a table representing Scripture usage in the *Antirrhetikos*. Without recounting all of the statistics, out of 492 verses in this work, 91 are from Psalms (18.5 percent), 60 are from Proverbs (12.2 percent), 13 are from Ecclesiastes (2.6 percent), and 20 are from Job (4.1 percent). That means out of 492 verses, 151 are from either Proverbs or Psalms, for a significant 30.7 percent, not to mention other Scripture usage. Clearly Scripture is important to Evagrius' system of thought, specifically the Psalms. Dysinger is most likely showing the specific importance of psalm usage, but it makes the

129. Ibid., 129, 130, quotation on 130.

130. Ibid., 115.

131. Ibid., 119.

132. Ibid., 116–17.

133. Evagrius' *Thirty-three Ordered Chapters*, specifically chs. 6 and 14 (Evagrius, *Evagrius of Pontus*, 224–26).

134. Dysinger, *Psalmody and Prayer*, 131.

broader point that Scripture is quite important to Evagrius.[135] The use of the Psalms, however, is notable, and should be kept in mind as this study moves forward.

In addition to the Psalms, many other Scripture passages are referenced in the *Antirrhetikos*. The title of this work means "rebuttal." It is divided into eight sections, one for each of the thoughts. In it Evagrius cites different ways in which a thought works and then cites a Scripture reference to counter these various difficulties.[136] For example, in "The Fifth Treatise: Against the Demon of Anger," besides Psalms and Proverbs, many Scripture books are referenced, including: Genesis, Numbers, 2 Samuel, Song of Songs, Isaiah, Lamentations, Matthew, Luke, John, 1 Corinthians, Galatians, Ephesians, Philippians, Colossians, 1 Thessalonians, 1 and 2 Timothy, Philemon, James, 1 Peter, and 1 John.[137] In this one treatise, there are references to almost every genre of literature found in the Old and New Testaments. For example, he states, "Against the thought of false witness generated by anger. 'You shall not bear false witness against your neighbor' [Exod. 20:16]."[138] In another instance more relevant to this study, he writes, "Against the mind that stirs up battle in the intellect by means of the thoughts. 'A slave of the Lord must not be quarrelsome, but must be gentle toward everyone' [2 Tim. 2:24]."[139] His use of Scripture is broad and directly attacks many individual problems. Scripture is used as a weapon against the thoughts, in this case the thought of anger, in its many different facets. In total Evagrius presents about 500 situations/ Scriptural responses in the *Antirrhetikos*.[140]

Summary of Evagrius' Worldview

This chapter has presented the work of Evagrius in many of his writings, as well as the work of current Evagrian scholarship, in an attempt to create a base of knowledge from which to engage current thought in theology and cognitive science. Admittedly, and somewhat necessarily, reliant on

---

135. Ibid., 136–37.

136. Stewart, "Evagrius Ponticus," 66.

137. Ibid., 71–80, quotation on 71. This section comprises the pages of Stewart's translation of this part of Evagrius' *Antirrhetikos*.

138. *Antirrhetikos* 5.3 (ibid., 72).

139. *Antirrhetikos* 5.55 (ibid., 79).

140. Stewart, "Practices of Monastic Prayer," 8.

the textual work of Robert Sinkewicz, Evagrius' writings have been shown to be full of detail and structure in regard to the "thoughts" and ways of defeating them.

The presentation of a system that moves from contemplation of the material to the immaterial and ultimately to the Trinity is in view as the monk (or reader) battles with the *logismoi*. In the *Kephalaia Gnostika* Evagrius presents a symbolic journey for the monk, moving from Egypt, which represents evil, to the desert (practical life), to Judah (the contemplation of the material), to Jerusalem (the contemplation of the immaterial), to Zion, which represents the Trinity.[141] Although this study will focus mainly on Egypt and the desert, where moral evil and the battle against it is found, the latter stages of the journey are important to keep in view as they present the reasons for the battle and why Evagrius' methods work in his context, and why they have openings for dialogue in ours.

There are a couple major ideas that need to be gleaned from his work. First, one must determine what type of thought is affecting one's mind. Second, one must use prayer, Scripture, and physical action to defeat the thought. As one continues in this vein, the battles will be different, and the victories more profound, in the sense that a person moves toward knowledge of the Trinity, and a healthy mind.

In presenting Evagrius in such short chapter, I feel I have treated the monk unjustly, but for a theological study such as this it is impossible to recount his many admonitions and their interpretation. For now we must leave Evagrius behind and move forward to present a hermeneutic in order to properly bring his work into the twenty-first century as well as present a system of how evil might be understood in a larger, mythical sense. For this we turn to the work of Pierre Hadot and Paul Ricoeur.

141. Sinkewicz, introduction to *On the Eight Thoughts* (Evagrius, *Evagrius of Pontus*, 69).

three

A Discussion of Evil and
a Recovery of Evagrius

NOW THAT A DISCUSSION of Evagrius' worldview regarding the
thoughts has been presented, it is helpful to connect Evagrius'
cosmos with that of the twenty-first century. This chapter presents a
discussion of evil, specifically moral evil, in conjunction with the work
of Pierre Hadot and Paul Ricoeur. First, a discussion of evil will lay the
foundation for further work on Evagrius, evil, and cognitive science, as
well as present some key concepts that are germane to an overall discussion of evil. This will not be comprehensive, but will raise some important
overarching themes regarding evil. The work of Hadot helps to present
Evagrius in his own context, showing his connection to Greek philosophy and ascetic practice, and will help the reader better understand his
cosmological worldview. Lastly, the work of Ricoeur discusses how evil is
described through symbol and myth, allowing this study to further show
how cognitive science is linked to myth-making and brain function. In
addition, Ricoeur's discussion of the symbols of evil can be linked back to
a discussion of Evagrius' work on the thoughts. Therefore, the goal of this
chapter is twofold: to connect Evagrius' work with a historical context in
order to better understand it, and to present a discussion on the concepts
and mythologies surrounding a conversation about evil, which are key to
a discussion of moral evil as related to Evagrius' thoughts.

Introduction to a Discussion of Evil

Although the preceding chapter presented Evagrius' writings on the thoughts, before moving forward it is necessary to present a discussion on evil, moving into the topic of moral evil, which is closely related to the thoughts. In this study, the reader should also be aware that I am writing from the perspective of Christian theology. In certain instances, there are alternative views that may have need to be addressed were this a comprehensive discussion on evil. However, due to the nature of this project, it is best to state this presupposition up front in order to focus on the task set before us.

What Is Evil?

First, evil must be defined, if only in a general sense, to raise some key concepts germane to a discussion of evil in order to better understand the conclusions of this work in its entirety. Before asking "What is evil?" a second question might be "Does evil exist?" If one does not know whether evil exists, there may be no need to know what it is. For Evagrius, it would seem the answer is that yes, there is evil, and most theologians would agree. In looking at the other question, "What is evil?" one sees that from Augustine and his view of original sin, to modern thinkers who might redefine evil, human beings look for ways to explain why certain events happen. One might see these events as evil or not, but for purposes of this study, evil will be treated as a reality. In a brief overview such as this, it is helpful to describe evil from biblical, theological, and cognitive viewpoints.

As one of the major sources of Christian doctrine and authority, the Bible is a good place to begin when constructing a theological perspective on evil. Evil is found early in the book of Genesis, whether one sees it in the Adamic account of 2:4b—3:24 or the first murder in chapter 4. Cain murders Abel and is accountable to God for his actions. This sets up a formula of a person acting improperly (evil) and answering for his actions. This pattern of behavior is typical of the Old Testament writers. Similar events transpire, and decisions are made by individuals, as well as the nations of Israel and Judah, which result in consequences, including the capture and diaspora of the peoples of these nations. The Old Testament law presents at least one method for making right these evils/sins. From the traditional Christian viewpoint, this culminates in the atoning death of Jesus Christ for the sin of humankind. Humanity has been separated from God by their sin and must be reconciled. Paul Tillich's concept of estrangement is also helpful in describing humanity's separation from God from a somewhat different perspective.[1] It is obvious that I have begun to use the terms sin and evil somewhat interchangeably, and from a biblical point of view I believe this to be a fair assessment.[2] Evil is judged by a transcendent God, who is also immanent, reaching the culmination of this immanence in the person of Jesus Christ.[3]

Looking at evil from a more theological (and philosophical) point of view, evil becomes a more theoretical problem to be solved. The question of theodicy is fundamental to discussions about evil. The three maxims

1. Evil exists

2. God is all-powerful

3. God is totally good

constitute a logical problem as to how all three might be true.[4] In most cases, the first of these three is assumed to be true. There are cases where these are redefined or logically twisted to make all three true, but most often the second maxim is dropped out, as many Christian theologians do not want to engage a God who is not totally good or loving. Therefore, for the most part, theology assumes that evil exists. In an attempt, therefore, to avoid attributing this evil to God, many theologians have reinterpreted traditional understandings of God, rather than changing their understanding of evil as a true entity (however, some may choose to take the latter pathway). I hold that evil must be independent of God, but in all fairness, it is clear that God must allow evil if he is omnipotent, because of his absolute power. There is some appeal here to a free will argument, which states that God created all things "good" in accord with the Genesis account, but due to the corrupt will of humans, it has become evil or at

1. Tillich, *Systematic Theology* 2:44–45. On 45 Tillich notes, "Estrangement is not a biblical term but is implied in most of the biblical descriptions of man's predicament."

2. There should be a distinction made between evil and sin in broader theological discussion, however. Sin typically refers to a specific doctrinal concept, while evil usually is a broader, umbrella term, covering many types of bad things. Sin is a subset of evil.

3. It is also worth noting that God is viewed as immanent in the Old Testament many times, for example, in the stories of Adam, Noah, and Abraham, who all had personal relationships with God.

4. This is at the fore in Hick, *Evil and the God of Love*, 3.

least opened the door to evil. This however, causes problems when compared to the biblical account, in lieu of the serpent, as well as the scientific account, in which evolutionary process contains brutalities that many would consider evil.

Among the sciences, it is hard to hold this view as just mentioned. The evolutionary process is full of suffering and death, where nature is, as Tennyson states, "red in tooth and claw."[5] Clearly if one is to respect the scientific findings on the origins of the universe/earth, one must rethink ideas of evil and sin in light of traditional theological categories. Some do this by looking at the biblical accounts more mythically or literarily while still holding traditional themes. Some reject the scientific worldview, substituting their own brand of "science." In most academic communities, the former is preferred, and in order to be scientifically honest, it seems best. Without rehashing the battles within the creationist/evolutionist controversies, it is clear that one must be careful not to hold to strict literalism, lest traditional theological themes fall like a house of cards. Another branch of the sciences, cognitive science, informs us of how evil is formed and experienced in the mind/brain. This can lead into a discussion on moral evil, the topic of the next subsection. If people are hardwired for evil, are their actions truly "evil"? Does this make their actions sinful? The natural sciences can tell us if something is natural, but does this make it acceptable? Science raises these questions and they must be considered when creating a theology of evil.

The previous three paragraphs have outlined some of the considerations in creating a Christian theory of evil. I think in constructing a conception of evil, presenting several maxims may be more helpful than coming up with a concise definition. Evil is amorphous, and its definition must take on a similar character.

First, whatever evil is, *it is something to be fought against and defeated*. Evil, whether one defines it as the condition of a starving child, an inherent taint in the human condition, or a personal devil, is something that must be overcome. This falls in line with almost any Christian conception of evil, whether traditional or progressive, conservative or liberal. There are few that would criticize this maxim, as anyone who is willing to admit that evil exists would want to defeat it, whether this be by better education or temporal intervention by God.

5. Quoted from Livingston, *Modern Christian Thought* 1:250; see 250–51.

Second, *evil must not be directly attributable to God.* Despite the evidence of evil and suffering in the world, one should not throw out the idea of a good, loving God.[6] A God who will suffer with humanity and provide a temporal and eschatological defeat of evil is better than a God who endorses such evil, thus isolating human beings. It would be better to have no God than a God who delights in the sufferings of humankind. Also worth noting here is the fact that evil cannot be co-existent with God because then evil itself is raised to the position of another Deity. In other words, evil is not eternal. According to some traditional Christian theology, it does predate the Genesis narrative, thus accounting for Satan. Therefore it can and must be overcome as the previous maxim states. It also assumes that one believes in a loving God, who would not have evil as part of his nature.

Third, *evil must be viewed as contingent.* Evil is not something that human beings, as finite creatures, can fully define. Is the tragic death of a child an evil event? Clearly. But what if that child was sacrificed for the salvation of ten children? Would it still be viewed as evil? Although tragic, many would view this as a selfless act for the greater good, if not a heroic one. Clearly, circumstances often times decide whether something is deemed evil or not. From the viewpoint of Christian eschatology, evil must also be contingent because ultimately it will be defeated. Even if one does not hold to Christian theology, both naturalistic thought and secular philosophical thought could support this maxim. In naturalistic evolution, the "evils" that one encounters at each stage in time are changing and left in the past, at least in many cases, and thus are time-bound and contingent. Evil could be viewed as unending for the naturalistic thinker, however this could also be turned around to state that these events are not evil in the first place. What I mean by this is that the events are treated as "natural" and thus not as a radical departure from the ideal.

Fourth, *evil can be a moral failure.* This is the topic of the next subsection, but is important to a definition of evil. It relates directly to the broader topic of this book. Sometimes the workings of the mind malfunction for whatever reason, whether willful or not, and can lead to moral

6. Although this also could have been addressed earlier, how one defines love also plays a major role in how one views the theodicy question. Thanks to Robert A. Cathey for raising this point at my field examinations on March 31, 2008 at the Lutheran School of Theology at Chicago.

evil.[7] This is a more difficult maxim to define because what is evil for one (e.g., adultery), may be normal behavior for another. Morality is a relative concept for many, and is dismissed by others, but since this is a contingent statement to begin with, it can be true if one accepts any form of morality.

Fifth, *evil is a real entity and cannot be overcome by humanity alone.* This must be stated in opposition to those who believe that evil might be overcome by education or that evil is only the fear of death.[8] Although understanding both of these interpretations of evil may be helpful in overcoming some contingent evils, evil is too great an enemy for humanity to overcome on its own. Reinhold Niebuhr was correct to state that "modern liberal Protestant interpretations of human nature and human destiny stand in as obvious contradiction to the tragic facts of human history . . . as the more secular interpretations by which modern culture has been chiefly informed."[9] The facts of history are too stark to hold to belief in the defeat of evil by human action alone. The history of Christian theology is based on this premise. For a theology of evil to be truly Christian, it must hold to this fifth maxim because humanity is part of the problem. Reinhold Niebuhr is again helpful here, as evidenced in his concept of transcending the self in faith "to know that an ultimate word may be spoken against him; but he cannot himself speak that word."[10] Humans can be aware of evil, but cannot actually overcome this same evil on their own. For the naturalist who is not a Christian, this maxim still holds if one so inclines to believe that evil does indeed exist. Humanity is clearly limited in its ability to defeat evil and must receive help, whether this be from God, other creatures, or natural processes.

In the above five maxims there is also one implicit maxim that I have alluded to: *evil will be defeated eschatologically by God.*[11] If evil predates humanity, but is not eternal, and humanity cannot defeat evil alone,

---

7. Ashbrook and Albright, *Humanizing Brain*, 157–58. This will be addressed in more depth in chapter 4.

8. Cooper, *Dimensions of Evil*, 102–3, 131. These pages mention the work of Sigmund Freud and Ernest Becker.

9. Reinhold Niebuhr, *Nature and Destiny of Man* 1:299.

10. Ibid., 2:25–26. Niebuhr is extremely helpful for a discussion of evil and the necessity of Christ, but due to the nature of this study, his thought is alluded to only briefly.

11. This point was raised by Robert A. Cathey in reference to the maxims I presented at my field examinations at the Lutheran School of Theology on March 31, 2008.

God must eventually defeat evil. This is the hope of Christian theology. Without this hope, Christianity falls short of its fullness, leaving a vacuum that renders it impotent.

One more major distinction that needs to be made is that evil should be differentiated from sin, at least partially. Sin usually refers to a taint within humanity or in the plural, a "wrong" action or thought by a person or collective of persons. The Old Testament idea of "missing the mark" is helpful here. In that sense it could be a breaking of a moral code or divine fiat or relationship, such as Paul Ricoeur's use of the term in referring to breaking the Covenant.[12] In contrast, evil can be seen as an entity pre-existent to creation, as might be exemplified by the story of Lucifer, or as nothingness or the "shadow side" (as in Karl Barth).[13] Sin is a human endeavor, evil is universal. Sin takes place in the commission of a grievous act, or the omission of a necessary act. This distinction is important as one discusses evil and sin, especially since moral evil can often refer to sin. To put it mathematically, sin is a subset of evil.

In summary, one can see how these maxims, as well as a distinction between sin and evil, are helpful for defining evil. Although in this discussion it is apparent that I have described more of what evil is not than what it is, evil is clearly something to be fought against. Otherwise it is a theoretical exercise that leaves the speaker no nearer to practicing the "good": the kindness, the peace, and the joy of Christianity.

Moral Evil

Now that a general discussion of evil has been presented, it is helpful to look specifically at moral evil, which is related more closely to Evagrius' eight thoughts. When looking at a list of the thoughts, most of them refer in some way to a kind of moral evil that must be combated and controlled. This is important in connecting moral evil to the larger entity of evil because the thoughts (or moral evil in general) cause weakness in a person's will. This leads to self-destruction, as well as the harming of others, which can lead to larger societal evil and a weakening of the social fabric, thus making evil more acceptable and easily accessible. Moral evil does not only affect an individual, although that is where it often starts.

12. Ricoeur, *Symbolism of Evil*, 50–51. He also mentions "missing the target" (ibid., 72).

13. Schwarz, *Evil*, 163–64, referring to Barth's "shadow side."

It is just one branch of the larger topic of evil, which can lead to more violent and harmful results.

As Terry Cooper describes it, in the early twentieth century (and even today), societal evil became more the focus in theologies of sin and evil. Later on, the idea of personal sin did make a resurgence in writers such as Karl Barth, Paul Tillich, and Reinhold Niebuhr. The idea of sin being "rooted in our anxious finitude and misused freedom" in the Kierkegaardian way did make a comeback.[14] It is with these authors that it is imperative to state that the concept of moral evil in the individual person must not be lost. Instead of focusing on societal evil as the structures that cause people to sin, which is certainly worthwhile, I would argue that overcoming the sinful will of the individual is of the utmost importance in engaging moral evil. Some forms of government and economic structures are clearly more fertile ground for evil than others, but the root of the problem is still seated in the will of the individual. This bears a bit of explication. Structures certainly set the context for which individuals make decisions for good or for ill. Ultimately, however, the individual makes a choice whether to commit moral evil or not. While structures make the problem larger and more difficult, the individual still holds a great deal of responsibility, otherwise a "the structure made me do it" defense holds sway. Is this not the sort of argument Nazi war criminals used when arguing for the cause of their actions? The point I am making is not whether structures are sinful or not, but rather to place the ultimate responsibility on the individual's will. Communities can enforce good or bad behaviors, but it is still up to the individual whether honorable choices are made. If all persons within a sinful structure choose moral good, the structure ultimately holds no power.

This brings up a question for the study as a whole. If one holds that evil cannot be overcome by humans on their own, or that evil is a real entity that must be overcome by God, how can Evagrius' work on the thoughts hold merit? Is it not the individual overcoming evil by a series of disciplines and prayers? The main distinction to be made is that in the Evagrian system prayer and Scripture are practiced by the follower of God. Some may argue that a person cannot fight evil on her own, and this is linked to a broader harmatiology/soteriology, but in this study on Evagrius, he is speaking of the path of the monk, already a follower of

---

14. Cooper, *Dimensions of Evil*, 213.

Christ, and hence filled with the Spirit of God. It is important to make this distinction for both Evagrius and for modern Christians. Within a Christian framework, the battle to live a moral life is accomplished with the help of God, and not outside of God. However, for the one who does not accept a Christian worldview, this attention to Scripture and prayer to combat evil thoughts will not hold the same force. The question of moral evil is also (at least partly) nuanced for the non-Christian, as foundations for morality may be disputed.

At this time it is best to move forward in order to connect Evagrius to the present day by better understanding his context. The preceding discussion of evil, specifically moral evil, is meant to raise some of the questions and issues that may be related to the broader topic of evil and allow the reader to see some of this author's theological commitments as the study moves forward. These commitments will allow the reader to better understand the conclusions drawn from this discussion, especially in chapter 5.

Recovering Evagrius from His Context

Now that evil has been addressed in a broader theological context, it is necessary to move back to a discussion of Evagrius' context. For this the work of Pierre Hadot is especially relevant, along with other supporting authors. First, it is necessary to discuss Hadot's broader research on Greek philosophy before linking it directly with Evagrius Ponticus, who he does discuss briefly in some of his texts.

Philosophy as a Way of Life

This subsection is named after the title of one of Hadot's books, and this is also a major theme in his research. In addition to this text, his work *What Is Ancient Philosophy?* will be of specific importance. Hadot's research presents ancient philosophy within its own context, helping the modern reader to understand how the ancient world viewed it. Philosophy was more than just a theoretical endeavor for the ancients. It was something they were immersed in fully. Hadot describes it thus: "philosophical discourse must be understood from the perspective of the way of life of which it is both the expression and the means. Consequently, philosophy *is* above all a way of life . . ."[15] Since the time of Socrates, the way one lives does not emerge from philosophical thought, but is something that is interrelated from the beginning. "Philosophical discourse, then, originates in a choice of life and an existential option—not vice versa . . . this choice and decision are never made in solitude."[16] Thus the philosophical school is related to a wholesale lifestyle choice.[17] The idea that philosophy is solely a theoretical endeavor surfaced in the Middle Ages and carried forward.[18]

First, it is essential to make this distinction about the definition of philosophy for the ancients as opposed to current readers. Philosophy for the ancient Greeks was more than just mental exercise; it transformed the whole person. In fact during the whole of antiquity, philosophy was viewed in this manner. It was "a mode of life, and a technique of inner living."[19] Hadot goes on to state that the fact that Christianity did present itself as a philosophy affirmed this belief. Echoing Justin Martyr, he writes that since "to do philosophy" meant "to live in conformity with the law of reason," the Christians were philosophers who "lived in conformity with the law of the Logos—divine reason."[20] Christianity needed to show itself as fitting in with the prevailing concept of philosophy as a way of life. Hadot makes the case that this was done by borrowing elements from some of the prevalent philosophical schools. For example, the Logos was shown to correspond to the cosmic reason of the Stoics and the intellect of Plato and Aristotle.[21] This proves important in reading the system of Evagrius Ponticus, which has a focus on the intellect.

The Middle Ages changed everything, as scholasticism took hold with the advent of universities, and philosophy was made to be merely the "'servant of theology.'" No longer were people being trained to be fully developed persons. They were trained as specialists, by specialists. The spiritual exercises, which were a vital part of ancient philosophy, became an important missing piece, thus changing the whole of how it

15. Hadot, *What Is Ancient Philosophy?*, 3–4.

16. Ibid., 3, including the paraphrase above this quotation.

17. Ibid.

18. Ibid., 6.

19. Hadot, *Philosophy as a Way of Life*, 269, for both the quotation and the assertion that the nature of philosophy did not change throughout antiquity.

20. Ibid. Justin is referenced in 275n24.

21. Ibid.

was approached.[22] Spiritual exercises were a key ingredient to the ancient philosophical system in large part because passions were deemed the cause of suffering and disorder in the world. People's ability to live was hampered by the worries that controlled their lives.[23] Human freedom was of the utmost importance in allowing for evil to be avoided and good attained, thus moral good and evil are necessary choices of the will in this worldview. Philosophy's goal was to educate people in this attainment of the good.[24]

At least in some incipient form, spiritual exercises likely predate Socrates, and later on they became an inherent part of philosophical life. Although specific written works did exist, most of it was spread by oral teachings.[25] Later on one finds that "Platonic dialogues are model exercises." They show what an ideal dialogue looks like. One must dialogue with the self, which Hadot describes as doing battle with oneself.[26] He goes on to state that "Platonic dialogue corresponds exactly to a spiritual exercise" because it " turns the soul away from the sensible world, and allows it to convert itself towards the Good."[27] Although coming centuries later, this sounds very much like the spiritual disciplines found in Evagrius.

Within the discussion on spiritual exercises, meditation takes a prominent position. Meditation is "the 'exercise' of reason . . . . Greco-Roman philosophical meditation is not linked to a corporeal attitude but is a purely rational, imaginative, or intuitive exercise that can take extremely varied forms."[28] Hadot goes on to explain that theory and practice are intimately linked in regard to meditation. Theory does not stand alone, but is used in practice.[29]

The ancient philosophical schools saw themselves as holders of an ancient truth passed down from the divine, and hence holders of *the* truth. This was important in the second century, as pagans and Christians

22. Ibid., 270, including quotation.

23. Ibid., 83.

24. Ibid.

25. Hadot, *What Is Ancient Philosophy?*, 179–80, 188, respectively. Hadot states on 188, "Treatises entitled *On Exercise* did exist, but they are now lost. Under this title, we have only a brief treatise by the Stoic Musonius Rufus."

26. Hadot, *Philosophy as a Way of Life*, 91.

27. Ibid., 93.

28. Ibid., 59.

29. Ibid., 60.

argued over which of their systems was more ancient, using Moses and Plato as examples in this back-and-forth discussion. In this world, "error" was thought to come about by, for example, bad exegesis or mistranslations, hence the truth was in the text, but had to be understood and transmitted properly.[30]

Hadot on Evagrius

So it is clear that philosophy for the ancient Greeks was a way of life. This was the world of philosophy into which Evagrius entered in the fourth century. Hadot specifically discusses this Christian world in the two texts I am here engaging.

Evagrius came out of the Cappadocian tradition, which followed on the work of Clement of Alexandria and Origen. The fourth-century desert fathers saw the monasticism of the period as a "'Christian philosophy.'"[31] In the first and second centuries, Christian schools of an exegetical nature were appearing, and Origen and the teacher of Clement of Alexandria are examples of founders of these schools. Greek philosophy already contained a form of systematic theology begun by Plato in *Timaeus* and later developed by Aristotle in *Metaphysics*, therefore Christian philosophy was able to follow this model. Hadot goes on to state that it was less a parallel of this pagan theology, but more similar with philosophy because Christianity was a way of life, as was Greek philosophy.[32] By the fourth century, Christianity had acquired spiritual exercises and took on a different style than in its earlier years. Hadot finds this significant because it shows that "Christianity was able to be assimilated to a philosophy" because philosophy was itself a way of living.[33]

This is seen specifically in the Cappadocian Fathers. For example, Stoicism and Platonism are found in the works of Basil the Great, and Gregory Nazianzen speaks about "'concentration in oneself,'" which is a

---

30. Ibid., 74. Also worth noting is that most philosophical texts from the Hellenistic period have been lost. He notes that our view of the ancient world might be quite different if many of these texts remained. Hadot cites the example of the Stoic philosopher Chrysippus, who wrote seven hundred works, of which only a few fragments remain. This discussion is found in ibid., 53.

31. Hadot, *What Is Ancient Philosophy?*, 241–42, quotation on 241.

32. Ibid., 239, 240, covering all material subsequent to the previous note.

33. Hadot, *Philosophy as a Way of Life*, 129–30, quotation on 130.

prevalent theme in the Stoics and Neoplatonists: attention to the self.[34] These are Evagrius' mentors. Hadot specifically mentions that Evagrius "was more influenced by Platonic and Neoplatonic conceptions," specifically mentioning the tripartite division of the soul in reference to virtue.[35] The influence of Greek philosophy was clearly a part of the Cappadocian ethos.

From this background, one sees the importance of Greek philosophy in the life and works of Evagrius. His system corresponds to the "three parts of philosophy: ethics . . . physics, and theology." Evagrius parallels this to his three-part system. "[E]thics corresponds to *praktike*, physics to 'the Kingdom of Heaven' . . . and theology corresponds to 'the Kingdom of God,' which is the knowledge of the Trinity." In Porphyry, virtues are used "to dominate the passions," and at the level of theoretical virtues they reach a "full *apatheia* and perfect separation from the body." Hadot states that this corresponds to Evagrius' second level of contemplation, which is prior to the final contemplation of God.[36] Hadot defines apatheia as "the complete absence of passions—a Stoic concept taken up by Neoplatonism."[37] In sum, quoting Evagrius, he states, "Thus, Evagrius sums up his thought in these terms: 'Christianity is the doctrine of Christ our Savior. It is composed of *praktike*, of physics, and of theology.'" He goes on to state that *apatheia* is essential to both Evagrian metaphysics and monastic spirituality.[38] As mentioned previously, the passions were an important part of Greek philosophy because they caused suffering. The Evagrian system also follows from this concept, and the passions are very much at the root of moral evil in his system of the thoughts. For Evagrius, *apatheia* is the means used to attain "the death for which the philosopher-monk is in training," which is separation from the body through the lack of passions.[39]

Looking specifically toward the ascetic practices, for the monks, "asceticism was understood as participation in the Passion." Ascetic practices followed from the spiritual exercises of Greek philosophy, but they also

34. Hadot, *What Is Ancient Philosophy?*, 242, 243.

35. Ibid., 245.

36. Hadot, *Philosophy as a Way of Life*, 137, including all above quotations in this paragraph.

37. Ibid., 136.

38. Ibid., 137–38.

39. Hadot, *What Is Ancient Philosophy?*, 247.

were formed into a specifically Christian system. "Christian philosophers tried to Christianize" philosophical themes found in secular philosophy. Monks saw Christ in the human person, which gave them reason to control passions such as anger. Christian ascetic practices were described by language used by both the Christian Scriptures and secular philosophy.[40]

Evagrius also paralleled ancient philosophy in the format used in his writings. The short sentences that were used to remember various maxims were also used in ancient philosophy. Two specific literary genres were especially useful to monks due to their need to memorize and meditate: *Apophthegmata* and *Kephalaia*. They preceded the desert fathers and are found in ancient philosophy. *Apophthegmata* are well-known sayings spoken in specific situations. *Kephalaia* "are collections of relatively short sentences, usually grouped into 'centuries.'" Examples are found in Marcus Aurelius and Porphyry.[41]

In addition, Evagrius specifically picks up a few other ideas that are found in ancient philosophy. One is that of dreams. Plato and Zeno noted "that the quality of our dreams allows us to judge the spiritual state of our soul." This is picked up by Evagrius in the *Praktikos*.[42] Second, and more importantly, is the idea of fighting one passion with another, which is found in Cicero's *Tusculan Disputations*.[43] This is an important point, as Evagrius uses ancient philosophical method in defeating the moral evil found in the passions.

It is clear that in Evagrius' writings both form and content have roots in ancient philosophy. It has been established that prior to Evagrius, Christianity was viewed as a philosophy—a way of life. Evagrius followed in this tradition, as did many other early church fathers.

---

40. Ibid., 248, 249, including quotations in this paragraph. In regard to controlling the passions, I gleaned this from Hadot's example on page 248: "Similarly, the monk saw Christ in every human being: 'Aren't you ashamed to get angry and speak evil of your brother? Don't you know that he is Christ, and that it is Christ you are harming?' Here, the practice of the virtues takes on a completely different meaning."

41. Hadot, *Philosophy as a Way of Life*, 133. Marcus Aurelius' *Meditations* and Porphyry's *Sentences* are the examples Hadot states as types of *Kephalaia*.

42. Ibid., 135, 143. Endnote 80 on page 143 states that this comes from the *Praktikos*.

43. Ibid., 135. This is similar to the to the point Evagrius makes about using one mental representation to replace another in *On Thoughts* 24 (Evagrius, *Evagrius of Pontus*, 169–70).

Discussion of Evagrius' Recovery and Context

It is worth noting that in addition to Hadot's work, Jaroslav Pelikan also discussed the Cappadocians in the context of Greek culture.[44] He brings forth the important point that the Cappadocians were centered in Classical Greek culture, but also were "intensely critical of that tradition."[45] Evagrius was coming from a world that was rooted in the ancient philosophical traditions, yet was also quite critical of them. The Cappadocians blamed heresies on those who marred Christian truth with the philosophy of the heathens. It was a sort of irony, that Gregory of Nyssa, who was a neopla-tonist, could also attack Eunomius for "trying 'to make Plato's theory a doctrine of the church.'"[46] So in an ironic way, the Cappadocians used the tools of ancient philosophy to critique this same ancient philosophy.

This point taken from Pelikan also serves to enforce Hadot's view-point that Christianity was accepted as a philosophical system because it was seen as a way of life. Thus it might be said that the actual belief system of the Greeks was rooted in this underlying definition of philosophy. This kind of dichotomy allowed the Cappadocian Fathers to use ancient philo-sophical method while critiquing the actual beliefs within these systems.

In addition to Evagrius' philosophical background, he was influ-enced by the monastic tradition. Michael O'Laughlin writes that Evagrius was influenced by an Origenistic philosophical tradition among monks that predated his arrival in Egypt. So he was actually "representative of Egyptian monastic theology, as well as being an original thinker." Alexandrian theology already had a "speculative and experimental form" that predated Evagrius.[47] O'Laughlin, referencing Samuel Rubenson, lists eighteen doctrinal points where Evagrius draws on Antony, including "Purification through asceticism being essential to acquiring knowledge and returning to unity."[48] In discussion of these points, O'Laughlin men-tions that "concern over demonic interference is ultimately of pagan ori-gin, but was certainly further shaped in monastic circles prior to Evagrius." He goes on to reference Guillaumont and Bunge, two well-known Evagrian

---

44. Because the work of Hadot has laid a solid foundation to move forward with this study, little will be said about Pelikan's book *Christianity and Classical Culture*.

45. Pelikan, *Christianity and Classical Culture*, 9.

46. Ibid., 18.

47. O'Laughlin, "Closing the Gap," 345.

48. Ibid., 345, 347–48, quotation on 348.

scholars who note that Evagrius drew on Antony for his demonology. It is worth mentioning that O'Laughlin does not agree with Rubenson on every point, but clearly shows his agreement that Evagrius and Antony are connected in a more than a cursory way.[49] So without pursuing this further, there is ample evidence that Evagrius' context was determined not only by the Greek philosophical tradition, but an established Egyptian monastic tradition.

In sum, it is clear that the theology that Evagrius received was filtered through the Greek philosophers, Origen, and the Cappadocians before finally reaching him. It went through a further filter of the Egyptian desert, proving that Evagrius is a bridge between the ancient philosophical usage in the Eastern fathers and the asceticism of the desert, which itself had roots in the spiritual exercises of ancient philosophy.[50]

Paul Ricoeur: The Symbols and Myth of Evil

Moving away from Evagrius and back to evil as a broader topic, the work of Paul Ricoeur is essential for understanding the representations our minds use for describing evil. First, it is necessary to take a look at his symbols of evil, which lay the foundation for discussion of the topic of evil. Second, a discussion of Ricoeur on the myths about evil will help to describe the historical myths that religions have used. Third, this section will present a discussion on Ricoeur's thought and how he relates to the overall argument of this study.

The Symbols of Evil

In the first three chapters of *The Symbolism of Evil*, Ricoeur introduces three symbols of evil: defilement, sin, and guilt. In attempting to describe the symbolic, he raises the key point that even "*the most primitive and least mythical language is already a symbolic language.*" For Ricoeur, "the preferred language of fault appears to be indirect and based on imagery." The abstract comes from this image-based conception.[51] This is important

---

49. Ibid., 349, including quotation.

50. This was noted previously in the discussion of Hadot. Another text that has some discussion on Evagrius and presents the context out of which he grew is Louth, *Origins of the Christian Mystical Tradition*.

51. Ricoeur, *Symbolism of Evil*, 9.

for conceiving of how our mind develops descriptions of evil. Ricoeur sees myth forming from symbol, with symbol being primitive, "spontaneously formed," and "immediately significant."[52] Symbols are primary, myths secondary, with gnosis following these two.[53] The discussion of symbol is at the core of how humanity forms ideas of evil.[54]

Defilement is the first symbol of evil. Ricoeur discusses it in terms of the impure. It is something that infects in an invisible way.[55] It places things into categories of either pure or impure and eventually "follows a distribution of the sacred and the profane which has become irrational for us." It is beyond one simple concept. Defilement can increase in intensity, depending on the action it is related to, as in the example of sexuality.[56] Ricoeur goes on to say that purity goes along with virginity, as sexuality with contamination. Sexuality has both a material and an immaterial component. There is material defilement, but he also states "that it is pre-ethical in character," and makes the case that if it were not symbolic in nature, there would be no way to correct it. The strong symbol involved in this example transfers to the birth of a child, who is the result of sexual action, and marriage rites seek to rein in this "universal impurity of sexuality."[57]

In this one example, the strength of defilement in the human consciousness is seen. Sexuality exemplifies the way in which humans relate to impurity, and shows how various methods are used to make the impure pure. Defilement is also an "ethical terror" for Ricoeur.[58] It is intimately linked to suffering. Illness, death, and suffering are all related to having sinned. For Ricoeur, reason and piety explain suffering in this way. When one places the responsibility for suffering on humanity by attributing

---

52. Ibid., 18.

53. Ibid., 9.

54. In *The Symbolism of Evil*, 20, Ricoeur discusses the origins of our philosophical beliefs. He states "Our philosophy is Greek by birth" and "the *encounter* of the Jewish source with the Greek origin is the fundamental intersection that founds our culture." This is important to note following a discussion of Pierre Hadot's work, in that the discussion of the symbols of evil also has many roots in the Greek and Hebraic traditions. The context of the language of evil also follows a similar path to the context for Evagrius' language.

55. Ibid., 25–26.

56. Ibid., 27–28, quotation on 27.

57. Ibid., 28, 29, quotations on respective pages.

58. Ibid., 29–33.

impurity to humanity, God keeps his innocence intact.[59] This connects back to the question of theodicy. If God is all good and all-powerful, yet evil exists, the blame for that evil must rest in outside sources, thus falling on humanity and the demonic. This does not solve the issue, but it does alleviate some of the blame that one would tend to place on the Deity. The other side to this is that the blame can fall on humanity, which can be a problem on an individual level. Sometimes people suffer due to evil and sinfulness in the world, even if it is not their own sin that caused it. Thus it is still possible to be a victim of suffering, yet not be responsible for it, nor attribute it to God. The suffering may come from another human source, a demonic source, or possibly be a product of natural evil.

There are a few important concepts about defilement that still bear mentioning for this study. One is that defilement is like a stain, but not actually a stain. Ricoeur writes that "it is a symbolic stain." However, Ricoeur states that the most important part is the fact that it is spoken into existence afterward. The stain is the symbol, but speech teaches us about impurity from stain.[60] This repeats the concept that the symbol is primary, and emphasizes what he later means when he states, "'The symbol gives rise to thought.'"[61] He reiterates that the West owes its descriptions of pure and impure to classical Greece.[62] This leads to the important observation that only in community and through the spoken word are purity and impurity defined, thus making stain defilement. For Ricoeur, without this human element, things are not defined as pure and impure, as in the example of hyena excrement left near a human tent.[63] In this example, the excrement has no meaning until it is assigned by humanity. The excrement left by the tent is just an act until deemed impure by the viewer. I would note, however, that within Christian tradition it is possible to understand defilement in the falling of angelic/demonic beings without any connection to humanity.[64] These spiritual beings are defiled

59. Ibid., 31–32.

60. Ibid., 35–36, quotation on 36.

61. Ibid., 348.

62. Ibid., 37.

63. Ibid., 40.

64. I should note that in this example it is still humanity attributing this defilement to the fallen angels, or demons, but this would also depend upon one's view of divine revelation. Therefore, this example may be better fitting under sin and makes for a nice transition to that term. The narrative about fallen angels is clearly more loaded toward defilement than a simple excrement left by a tent. Ricoeur's point is made, however.

in their disobedience to God apart from humanity. Perhaps this connects more with Ricoeur's second symbol, sin.

Sin begins in relation to the Covenant. The Covenant established in Judaism created this relationship between the Hebrews and God. For Ricoeur, Covenant refers to the covenant made between the Jews and God—Berit.[65] Covenant in the Hebrew, בְּרִית, refers to "a formal commitment made by one party to another party, or by two parties to one another; its seriousness is normally undergirded by an oath and/or rite undertaken before God and/or before other people."[66] There are many covenants found in the Old Testament, beginning with the Noahic and Abrahamic covenants. Over time more clarity was revealed about the covenant commitment between God and the people of Israel.[67] Here Ricoeur seems to be referring to this same covenant relationship that the people of Israel have with God. This is evident in his movement in the following two headings. They cover the prophets and the wrath of God in the breaking of the Covenant.[68] When the Covenant is broken, sin results. Ricoeur goes on to say that theism precedes sin, but is inclusive of both monotheistic and polytheistic beliefs, and states that this theism is prior to any theology.[69] In this way, sin is kept in a primitive form, before the baggage of later interpretation. At least this seems to be Ricoeur's intent. He attempts to keep these concepts as "types," not rooted in history, at least as much as possible.[70] At this point in his text the establishment of these symbols is most important, being that upon which myths are later built.

Because Ricoeur devotes a rather long section of his book to sin, let us focus on some key concepts. This is done in two parts: "Sin as 'Nothingness'" and "Sin as Positive."[71] In the first part, Ricoeur presents sin as a break from defilement, while still connecting back to it. Sin is like defilement as a reality, but different in that it is "primarily the rupture of a relation."[72] If sin is the breaking of a covenant, it is inherently defined in correlation to this covenant relationship. Because of this, it is impos-

65. Ricoeur, *Symbolism of Evil*, 50.
66. Goldingay, "Covenant, OT and NT," 767.
67. Ibid., 767–70, specifically 770.
68. Ricoeur, *Symbolism of Evil*, 54–70, headings begin on 54 and 63, respectively.
69. Ibid., 50–51.
70. Ibid., 50.
71. Ibid., beginning on 70 and 81, respectively.
72. Ibid., 70.

sible to discuss sin without also discussing redemption. He relates this
to the inability to speak of defilement without purification. Within this
discussion Ricoeur presents a few descriptors for sin flowing from the
Greek and Hebrew traditions. For the sake of space, I will briefly present
them without the etymological discussion. Sin can be described as missing the mark, "that of a tortuous road," rebellion, and the idea of going
astray or being lost. The first two can be combined to present something
of a straying from the proper path. The first meaning is analogous to the
well known ἁμάρτημα in Greek, or *peccatum* in Latin.[73] In all of these
descriptions of sin, the concept is formed in relation to something else,
enforcing the idea of the covenant relationship. This relationship aspect is
stressed even more when Ricoeur correlates the idea of pardon to that of
return, which he relates to the prophets of the Hebrew Scriptures.[74]

From this pardon-return connection, he moves into a discussion
of "sin as positive."[75] Ricoeur makes three points regarding the "'reality'
of sin" as opposed to the "'subjectivity' of the consciousness of guilt."[76]
First, the reality of sin allows the sinner to be penitent and repent for sins
that are actual—a breaking of the covenant. Second, sin is real "because
it cannot be reduced to its subjective measure"; it is both "personal *and*
communal." Third, sin is in the sight of God, not internal to oneself, as
with guilt.[77]

This reality juxtaposed with the more subjective guilt is essential in
looking at evil as a general topic, and especially relevant to this particular
study. Following the discussion on the reality of sin, Ricoeur states:

> The traits that we have just analyzed attest that this sin, "internal"
> to existence, contrary to the defilement that infects it from "with-
> out," is no less irreducible to consciousness of guilt; it is internal
> but objective. This first group of characteristics assures the phe-
> nomenological continuity between defilement and sin.[78]

73. Ibid., 71–73, quotation on 72.

74. Ibid., 77–80.

75. Ibid., 81.

76. Ibid., 82. Note: his chapter on guilt follows the one on sin and will be addressed
shortly.

77. Ibid., 82–84, quotations on 83.

78. Ibid., 86.

This is an important observation in relation to Evagrius' work in that his way of combating the demons moves ever inward in the same way the symbols of evil move inward, from defilement to sin to guilt.[79]

Following this discussion of sin, Ricoeur addresses the symbol of guilt. Guilt is placed in sequence with the other two symbols, defilement and sin, and is understood in a context of rupture followed by resumption. In rupture the guilty person emerges, and in resumption both sin and defilement come into play, and a paradox emerges: a person "who is responsible *and* captive," "responsible for being captive . . . the concept of the *servile will*."[80] Ricoeur calls the "consciousness of guilt . . . a veritable revolution in the experience of evil." It is beyond defilement, "an internal diminution of the value of the self." Consciousness of guilt reverses the person's approach to punishment. Where previously punishment was applied to a person, causing guilt, now consciousness of this guilt is the call for punishment and the need for restoration.[81] It is hard to see the transition from sin to guilt, but it is in the confession of sins that a person internalizes sin, and thus it becomes guilt.[82] This movement from sin to guilt is important because it opens the door for hope, for personal salvation. Ricoeur states that just as communal sin has indicated that there is no choice, individual sin, and hence, individual guilt, open the door for individual salvation.[83] This is an interesting movement, mainly because when it seems that things are more difficult for the individual, it is actually at that moment there is true hope.[84]

79. Before moving on to guilt, there are some notable concepts regarding the "pardon-return" pairing. There is a discussion of return that links to the idea of "'buying back.'" In connection with Greek philosophy, he finds this concept in Plato's *Phaedo*, where there is the proposition of trading passions for virtue (Ricoeur, *Symbolism of Evil*, 91). This discussion goes on for a bit, ultimately arriving at the conclusion that sin is possession, and pardon is that of buying back (ibid., 91–94, conclusion on 94). This lines up nicely with the Western Christian tradition, especially those who follow an Anselmian soteriology. In addition, Ricoeur links sin to blood. Connecting this back to the concept of pardon, he states, "the *symbolism of blood* constitutes the bond between the rite of expiation and the faith in pardon . . ." (ibid., 97). This again will fit with traditional Christian atonement theory.

80. Ibid., 100–101, quotations on 101.

81. Ibid., 102, including quotations following preceding note.

82. Ibid., 102–3.

83. Ibid., 105.

84. In a biblical sense, from a Christian perspective, this mirrors the juxtaposition of the Law of the Torah and the grace of Jesus Christ. In this comparison, it is through the

Within the discussion of guilt, Ricoeur specifically discusses scrupulousness, which is "the advanced point of guilt." At this point there is a "personal imputation of evil" as well as "the polarity of the just man and the wicked man."[85] Moving forward through a discussion of the Romans 7 passage, where Paul writes about the divided person, Ricoeur links scrupulousness with the curse of the law. It is in scrupulousness that "the attempt to reduce sin by observance becomes sin."[86] Emphasizing the movement from the outward to the inner, he draws on Paul's discussion of justice as starting from the transcendent and moving to the immanent. Salvation is truly understood personally once it has been "recognized" from the transcendent.[87] This connects back to the previously mentioned idea of personal sin allowing for personal salvation.

Ricoeur concludes the section on guilt with this statement:

> The last word, then, of a reflection on guilt, must be this: the promotion of guilt marks the entry of man into the circle of condemnation; the meaning of that condemnation appears only after the event to the "justified" conscience; it is granted to that conscience to understand its past condemnation as a sort of pedagogy; but, to the conscience still kept under the guard of the law, its real meaning is unknown.[88]

Guilt affects the person more so who has been "justified" and who is aware of his condemnation. This can be drawn out to include the Evagrian system. For the monk who is aware of his sin will have a greater battle with his conscience than one who is not under this condemnation. Don Ihde states, "Guilt and its symbolism complete this subjectivization of the experience of evil" [that sin began].[89] This reinforces the discussion alluded to in the paragraphs on sin, that there is a movement in symbol toward guilt that moves from the outward to the inner. As is evident, by becoming more subjective, the symbol becomes more internal, and more powerful. This is again stressed in Ricoeur's discussion of the three symbols. He states "that defilement becomes a pure symbol when it no longer

---

difficulty of the Law that hope comes from the visibility of our sin.

85. Ricoeur, *Symbolism of Evil*, 128.

86. Ibid., 143. Discussion of Romans 7 is found especially on 139–43.

87. Ibid., 147.

88. Ibid., 150.

89. Idhe, *Hermeneutic Phenomenology*, 111.

suggests a real stain at all, but only signifies the servile will."[90] Again this emphasizes the inner movement of fault.[91]

The "Evil Myths"

Following the discussion of the symbols of evil, Ricoeur presents a lengthy discussion of four myths: the chaotic creation, the tragedy myth, the Adamic myth, and "the myth of the exiled soul."[92] Prior to this, there is a discussion of the function of myth and its relation to the symbols previously mentioned.

The Symbolism of Evil presents three functions of myth. The first "is to embrace mankind as a whole in one ideal history." The human type is described in a uniform way in order to create a "type" of human. Adam is an example of this. Second, the experience of humankind is seen in its movement through history and "in recounting the *Beginning* and the *End* of fault." This is a function of universalizing experience. Third, myth functions as a way of explaining the paradox of humanity being ideally an innocent creature and the reality of humans being sinful and guilty creatures.[93] So in sum, myth functions to unify the person of humanity, the experience of humanity, and the nature of humanity. Ricoeur describes these as "concrete universality, temporal orientation, and . . . ontological exploration." He states that this three-way function of myth allows it to reveal truths "not reducible to any translation from a language in cipher to a clear language."[94] From there, he sets out to show that myth is a second-

90. Ricoeur, *Symbolism of Evil*, 154–55.

91. I have chosen to follow Ricoeur in using the term "fault" as using sin or guilt is difficult because of the specific meanings attributed to them in his discussion of symbol. An example of his use of fault is found at the bottom of ibid., 100. As an additional note, as much space as has been allotted to this discussion of Ricoeur's symbols, there is so much more to address that a separate study should really be allotted. One example of this is the "captivity-deliverance" link that Ricoeur presents under the heading of "Scrupulousness," stating, "That is why also the whole of the symbolism of sin and repentance is itself a 'historical' symbol that draws its 'types' from certain significant events (captivity-deliverance)." His "*ethical* monotheism" is historically rooted. Ibid., 119.

92. These are found in *Symbolism of Evil*, pt. 2, chs. 1–4. For the sake of space, only a brief discussion of these myths and their importance follows. Again, as with his symbols, there is much more to write on this. I would encourage readers of this book to be familiar with the work of Ricoeur.

93. Ibid., 162–63.

94. Ibid., 163.

ary function of the primary symbols of defilement, sin, and guilt. Thus myth must be viewed as both contained as "an expression in language" and "that in it the symbol takes the form of narration."[95] Ultimately, myth is meant to restore the wholeness that is already missing in primitive humanity. Early humanity is divided, and myth-making seeks restoration. It is "an antidote to distress." This division is caused by a realization of the differences between the human, the natural, and the supernatural, causing the human being to seek a restoration that can only be symbolic. "Myth-making is primordial, contemporaneous with the mythical structure, since participation is signified rather than experienced."[96]

The first myth, that of the chaotic creation, is the myth that describes a creation that is rooted in God's struggle with "'*chaos*'" in creating.[97] It is found in the Sumerian and Akkadian creation stories.[98] Specifically, the Gilgamesh epic deals with death, not sin. "[I]t is the quest for immortality that reveals mortality as fate. Evil is death."[99] The eschatology of creation is tied intimately with the initial creation. The chaos that God struggles with in creation, mirrors the evil that salvation overcomes—"*salvation is identical with creation itself.*"[100] Evil is not something "that upsets a previous order"; it is inherently a part of "the foundation of order." Evil is the "Enemy" of the initial creation—chaos, in the beginning, and "the King" who later destroys the wicked using "the same ambiguous power of devastation and of prudence that once upon a time established order."[101] Ricoeur follows with discussions of both the Hebrew King, which ultimately results in the need for the Adamic myth, and that of the Greek Titan, which in turn is later used in the three other mythic types.[102]

The tragic myth is found in many places, but is typified by the Greek tragedies.[103] In this type of myth there are two sides to the tragic: fate and human action. Suffering is shown to be an action that is set up to oppose

95. Ibid., 165, 166, quotation on 166.

96. Ibid., 167, 168, quotations on respective pages.

97. Ibid., 172.

98. Ibid., 175.

99. Ibid., 187.

100. Ibid., 172.

101. Ibid., 198.

102. Ibid., 198 and 206 begin the respective sections, 205 mentions the need for the Adamic myth, and 210 discusses the Titans in the other myths.

103. Ibid., 211.

fate. It is in this opposition to fate that suffering becomes tragic.[104] The only response to the tragic, i.e., the only form of salvation, is in sympathy for the tragic hero.[105] There is no true resolution to the tragic myth, the internal tensions are left up to a separate religious order for closure. The "tragic vision of the world excludes forgiveness of sins."[106] The reader or viewer of the tragic myth finds herself a part of the myth by connecting herself with the chorus. In this connection, the reader feels the fear and lamentation of the tragic hero. Salvation is ultimately found within the myth by "an aesthetic transposition of fear and pity by virtue of a tragic myth turned into poetry and by the grace of an ecstasy born of a spectacle."[107] Ricoeur states an example of a form of "tragic theology," quoting Lycurgus. In it, he describes demons attacking a man and taking away reason, therefore worsening his judgment.[108] This is perhaps an allusion to the judgment one has under the rule of the passions. The tragic myth has some indirect links to Evagrius' work in this way, due to its rooting in Greek philosophy.

The Adamic myth, which is best known to Christians, is the third in Ricoeur's presentation. The Adamic myth is the only myth that is "strictly anthropological." There are three characteristics that contribute to this. First, the myth relates the origin of evil to a human ancestor who is in the same state as current humans. Ricoeur is clear that the elevation of Adam's pre-fall state is not a biblical idea and not a part of the Adamic myth. Adam must be in the same condition as current humanity. He does state that this idea of a fall "is found in Plato," which is one reason this myth must not be called the "'The Myth of the Fall,' but 'The Adamic Myth.'"[109] Second, in the Adamic myth there is a distinctive beginning to evil as opposed to good. Ricoeur describes it as "a *radical* origin of evil" versus a "*primordial* origin of the goodness of things."[110] Third, the central figure, Adam, has other figures subordinated to him, i.e., the serpent and

---

104. Ibid., 221–22.

105. Ibid., 227.

106. Ibid., 229, 230, quotation on 230.

107. Ibid., 231.

108. Ibid., 226.

109. Ibid., 233, including all preceding quotations in this paragraph.

110. Ibid., 233, discussion continues on 234.

Eve, who are also responsible for the origin of evil, yet still do not take on the primary fault. The story is still arranged in relation to Adam.[111]

Following up on the third anthropological point above, there is a distinction between external and internal blame for evil. There is blame placed on the serpent by Eve when God asks her why she disobeyed. As Ricoeur says, "The artfulness of the excuse is that it puts temptation, which had been hovering on the border between the inside and the outside, completely outside. . . . we might say that the serpent represents the psychological projection of desire."[112] One might also say that Adam does the same thing by blaming Eve for his disobedience. Ricoeur goes on to state that the serpent represents something of the world and of humanity. It represents "the chaos *in* me, *among* us, and *outside.*"[113] This discussion is important to this particular study of Evagrius because of the dual temptation of the demons/thoughts that are both an internal and external struggle for the monk. Ricoeur states regarding this myth, "To sin is to yield."[114] This is the same idea found in Greek philosophy in regard to the passions. The passions must be controlled so that reason carries the day.

To add one more note to the discussion, he links the Adamic myth back to the ideas of repentance and pardon, previously discussed in the symbols.[115] Ricoeur states that pardon receives meaning through a person's participation in the original "type" of humanity—Adam. Otherwise it is only held internally.[116] Regarding repentance, it receives "the symbol of that universality," i.e., the Adamic myth, where the naming of a man—Adam—"makes explicit the concrete universality of human evil."[117]

---

111. Ibid., 234–35. Although this myth is central to Christianity and important in any Christian understanding of evil, it is not explicitly central to this study. Readers should already be familiar with arguments about the Genesis narrative, "the fall," and original sin. Because of this, even though Ricoeur does spend a good deal of text discussing this myth, only a few key points relevant to this study will be presented.

112. Ibid., 256–57, discussion and quote.

113. Ibid., 258.

114. Ibid., 259.

115. Ibid., 241, 274.

116. Ibid., 274.

117. Ibid., 241. There is much to be added to this discussion in the realm of systematic theology and the dialogue between science and theology. In addition to the points already mentioned, Ricoeur references Paul's discussion of sin in Romans 7 in *Symbolism of Evil*, 247–52. This discussion ends with a mention of Kant's work *Essay on Radical Evil*. There Ricoeur states, "man is 'destined' for the good and 'inclined' to evil; in this

The final myth is that of the exiled soul. In this myth there is a division of human beings into a soul and a body, focusing on the soul—where it came from and especially where it is headed. This myth is often blended with the Adamic myth to form a myth of the fall.[118] This is seen in the Christian tradition, especially in the patristic period, as is evidenced in the work of Origen and Evagrius. Ricoeur makes the salient point that all anthropological dualism is an attempt to rationalize this myth.[119]

The exiled soul is found in Greek philosophy and Ricoeur raises the question of whether this myth is a later construction created to be "pagan apologetics" against Christianity. In other words, does this myth draw on more ancient sources to create authority or is it truly ancient?[120] Whatever one accepts as the answer, it is clear that in the time of Evagrius Ponticus this myth was a part of the ethos. The idea of the exiled soul is seen in the works of Origen and the pre-existence of the soul.

It is clear that Ricoeur's four myths have influenced Christianity in many ways and are important to a Christian understanding of evil, specifically to understanding Evagrius' conceptions of evil from the fourth century. It is these myths and the symbols that precede them that are important in moving forward to understand how evil is viewed by the mind/brain and to the practical purposes of this study.

Discussion of Ricoeur

Now that the symbols of evil and the myths are understood, a few broader discussion points can be made. Ricoeur presents the key symbols of evil as well as the myths that historically have composed the origins of evil. In composing a Christian conception of evil they are quite valuable. Although *The Symbolism of Evil* is a more comprehensive approach,

---

paradox of 'destination' and 'inclination' the whole meaning of the symbol of the fall is concentrated" (ibid., 252). This discussion is relevant to a study concerning the will, sin, and evil, but as it is not as central to this particular study, I will leave it behind at this time. Evagrius focuses on a battle with moral evil, while this is central to a broader understanding of evil. It is foundational, but a much broader topic.

118. Ibid., 174. He does not use the term "Adamic" here, in favor of "the myth of the fault of a primeval man," but this seems to be what he is getting at. It makes sense, especially in the context of some patristic cosmologies.

119. Ibid., 279.

120. Ibid., 289–90, quotation on 290. The discussion of Greek philosophy in this section is vast and found throughout the whole chapter.

subsequent writings of Ricoeur raise some important points in a more concise presentation about where to move beyond this initial work.

In two separate published lectures, Ricoeur presents a multi-step approach to discussing evil.[121] He describes these steps as increasing in rationality. In his 1984 American Academy of Religion lecture, the stages are identified as follows: Myth, Wisdom, Gnosis and Anti-Gnostic Gnosis, and lastly Theodicy.[122] In the Lausanne lecture, there is a fifth, "The stage of 'broken' dialectic."[123] Let us engage a brief description of each.

Myth is "the first major transition from experience to language" and has been discussed in the previous section.[124] It is clearly an important piece of understanding evil. Second, wisdom answers the question "Why?" in more depth. While myth gives us "the consolation of order," wisdom takes the next step to address questions of why the situation of evil applies to everyone. The story of Job falls into this category.[125]

Third, the stage of "gnosticism and anti-gnostic gnosis" is the bridge from wisdom to theodicy. In this stage the Augustinian and Pelagian approaches to moral evil leave open the question of suffering, thus opening the door to theodicy questions.[126] In Augustine's response to Gnosticism, he drew on the philosophers and thus came up with a solution where evil was no longer substantive. The result was a need for the doctrine of original sin. This was in opposition to Pelagius, who Ricoeur describes as appearing "more truthful" in putting the responsibility on individual human beings.[127]

The fourth movement is that to the "*stage of theodicy*."[128] Theodicy has already been discussed briefly in this chapter, so let us move on to the fifth, which is "The stage of 'broken' dialectic."[129] Here Ricoeur engages

121. The two are entitled "Evil, a Challenge to Philosophy and Theology," a plenary address at the 1984 American Academy of Religion, and *Evil: A Challenge to Philosophy and Theology*, a recent publication coming from a 1985 lecture in Lausanne.

122. Ricoeur, "Evil, A Challenge," 635, 637–40. On 637 he mentions the increase in rationality with the levels. He calls the third stage "*The stage of gnosticism and anti-gnostic gnosis*" in *Evil*, 44.

123. Ricoeur, *Evil*, 59.

124. Ricoeur, "Evil, a Challenge," 637.

125. Ricoeur, *Evil*, 41–44.

126. Ibid., 44, 49, quotation on 44.

127. Ibid., 45–48, quotation on 48.

128. Ibid., 49.

129. Ibid., 59.

Barth's thought and the acceptance of a "'broken' theology" that "recognizes that evil is a reality that cannot be reconciled with the goodness of God and the goodness of creation."[130] Without rehashing the discussion, this, I believe, is one appropriate response to the question of evil and theodicy. For Ricoeur, this stage is the next step in engaging theodicy.[131]

These five stages are important in understanding where Ricoeur goes after discussing the symbols of evil. The next part of the lecture presents three responses to evil: thinking, acting, and feeling.[132] As with this study, Ricoeur makes a point to state that a discussion of evil should not just be theoretical. Ricoeur stands with me in stating that "evil is above all what should not be, but must be fought."[133] If one does not respond to evil, the explanation of it becomes useless. It is an impotent endeavor without action.

Moving back to the broader discussion relating Ricoeur's work on evil with the other aspects of this text, a few points should be raised. He is important to this broader study of Evagrius and cognitive science because he provides explanations for how humans create language to explain evil. In effect this is what Evagrius is doing, as well as what is done in some aspects of cognitive science. The symbols of evil are foundational to an understanding of the mind in that they give us language to express the mind's experience. They also give language to spiritual experiences in the life of the Christian.

Just as Ricoeur moves from defilement to sin to guilt and then from there builds the myths of the origins of evil, Evagrius blazed a trail that leads from outward spiritual disciplines to the ultimate in non-corporeal, inner meditation in reaching the place of God. I appreciate the approach that Ricoeur takes because it is clearly Christian, but also explains the feelings that human beings experience in contemplation of their own actions. In helping us understand myth and the mind's formation of it, Ricoeur's symbols are building blocks wherewith this study can move onward to cognitive science.

130. Ibid., 59, 60, quotations on respective pages.

131. Ibid., 59–64. The whole discussion is located here, and although interesting, is not directly relevant for this study. The summary of these five stages is helpful, however, in moving us to the last part of Ricoeur's essay.

132. Ibid., 64. This begins the section.

133. Ibid., 64, 66, quotation on 66. In the first maxim I present in defining evil earlier in the chapter, I state that "whatever evil is, *it is something to be fought against and defeated*."

Summary of Recovering Evagrius and the Myths/Symbols of Evil

This chapter has presented a bridge between the world of Evagrius and that of cognitive science. I have discussed evil as a broader topic, showing some of its complexities, while trying to find a practical viewpoint, i.e., one must battle evil. Pierre Hadot has helped us to understand that the Evagrian worldview had a definite philosophical context based in Greek philosophy. This philosophy was "a way of life" and allowed for an easier acceptance of the Christian worldview, due to its similar approach as a way of living. Finally, Paul Ricoeur has shown that evil needs a language to be expressed and this language begins with the symbols of evil. These symbols give rise to myth, and these myths give rise to further deliberation.

When speaking of the moral evil of Evagrius' eight thoughts, one must see the broader context of how evil is defined, while also seeing how Evagrius' cosmological worldview was put together. From this chapter, one can see that Evagrius was very much in line with the philosophers of ancient Greece, while also following the Cappadocian Fathers in their work. The philosophical influences on the desert monastics most likely also influenced Evagrius so that he received the influences of Greek philosophy both from Asia Minor and the Egyptian desert. This is clear from the previous section containing the recovery of Evagrius focusing on Pierre Hadot, and also referencing authors such as Michael O'Laughlin. The philosophy of ancient Greece was prevalent throughout the fourth century in different regions of Christianity.

In moving toward cognitive science, Ricoeur's symbols are helpful because they can help us to understand how the human person deals with the concept of evil, and also help us to understand how Evagrius' conceptions of evil fit into a modern, scientific worldview by building a bridge between these worlds. Enough has been said about this usage. Now it is time to move into a deeper study of relevant cognitive science.[134]

---

134. Ricoeur will also be revisited in the next chapter in his interaction with Jean-Pierre Changeux.

four

How the Mind Deals with Evil

Cognitive Science

B EFORE MOVING FORWARD INTO a discussion of modern cognitive science, and following on the heels of Hadot and Ricoeur's work, it may be beneficial to briefly discuss the work of William James. This will be followed by a discussion of the cognitive sciences as they pertain to myth making and evil. Then, a discussion of psychotherapy and Christian spirituality will follow. Lastly, I will present a summary and discussion of the cognitive sciences as they apply to this overall study. Multiple researches are relevant to this dialogue, and this chapter attempts to weave them together, drawing from the foundations already laid by Evagrius Ponticus and the philosophers of this study.

Some Foundational Matters in Cognitive Science

In laying a foundation for a discussion of cognitive science, a bit of background drawn from the views of William James will help to enrich the conversation. Along with this background, a review of the difference between brain and mind may also be helpful.

William James

In his *Varieties of Religious Experience*, James addresses at least three topics that are pertinent for this study: natural proclivities for religion, evil,
and mysticism.[1] In looking at James' presentation, a door is opened to observe very early cognitive science. In addition, he offers a link between the
philosophical tradition and modern discussions on evil and the brain.

In regard to a possible organic cause for religion, James argues
against those who argue that it cannot be more. He states:

> To plead the organic causation of a religious state of mind, then, in
> refutation of its claim to possess superior spiritual value, is quite
> illogical and arbitrary, unless one have already worked out in ad-
> vance some psycho-physical theory connecting spiritual values in
> general with determinate sorts of physiological change. Otherwise
> none of our thoughts and feelings, not even our scientific doc-
> trines, not even our *dis*-beliefs, could retain any value as revela-
> tions of the truth, for every one of them without exception flows
> from the state of their possessor's body at the time.[2]

James argued against the positivistic thinkers who from Darwinist roots
saw "the sciences providing a God's eye-view."[3] In his thinking this opens
the door to true epistemological honesty, away from a reliance on science
providing the only truth about human behavior and action.[4]

James goes on to discuss evil for the "healthy-minded": "Evil is a
disease; and worry over disease is itself an additional form of disease,
which only adds to the original complaint . . . . The best repentance is
to up and act for righteousness, and forget that you ever had relations
with sin."[5] He states that evil becomes a philosophical "difficulty" when
one admits that it is essential to one's being.[6] He then discusses people
who cannot get away from the suffering of evil, some who see evil as "a
mal-adjustment with *things*, a wrong correspondence of one's life with

1. James, *Varieties of Religious Experience*, Lecture 1: "Religion and Neurology" (7–25,
specifically 17), Lectures 6 and 7: "The Sick Soul" (103–31), and Lectures 16 and 17:
"Mysticism" (294–332), respectively.

2. Ibid., 17.

3. Hollinger, "James, Clifford," 69.

4. Ibid. Hollinger presents that James was possibly one of the first postmodern thinkers and introduced "epistemic humility" in a prophetic voice.

5. James, *Varieties of Religious Experience*, 103.

6. Ibid., 106.

the environment. Such evil as this is curable . . ." Others in this group see evil as "a wrongness or vice in his essential nature . . . which requires a supernatural remedy."[7] In looking at Evagrius' work, I would argue that both types of evil are in view, despite it seeming that only one or the other must be accepted. There is a plea to the supernatural in Evagrius, yet a set of disciplines that treats the "illness."

Lastly, James addresses mysticism. He lists four marks of a mystical experience. (1) "Ineffability": the experience must be impossible to explain in words. (2) "Noetic Quality": the experience must also be a state of knowledge, insight into truths that one cannot access otherwise. The next two are less visible, "but are usually found." (3) "Transiency": the state does not last very long, rarely longer than an hour or two. (4) "Passivity": the state is controlled by another power, not the will of the person experiencing the state.[8] Ultimately James suggests that higher mystical states offer us hypotheses into more truth. "The supernaturalism and optimism to which they would persuade us may, interpreted in one way or another, be after all the truest of insights into the meaning of this life."[9] This conclusion is notable as we move into a discussion of the work of d'Aquili and Newberg and Evagrius Ponticus because their mystical states tell us more about the human person.

James' approach to religious experience shows a movement from "healthy-mindedness, with his distinction between an involuntary and a voluntary or systematic healthy-mindedness, to sick soul and divided self, to conversion, saintliness, and mysticism." The progression follows the ideal of "evangelical religious experience." Interestingly, James is attracted by the spiritual battle of John Bunyan, which may hold use in discussion with Evagrius because of his use of warfare language.[10]

Discussing the Mind/Brain

Although this was done briefly in the first chapter, a review of how the terms "brain" and "mind" are defined may be helpful. The brain is the physical organ that resides in a person's head. It is physically responsible

7. Ibid., 108.

8. Ibid., 294–96.

9. Ibid., 331–32, quotation on 332.

10. Richard Niebuhr, "William James on Religious Experience," 225, including quotations.

for the actions of the person. In the biological part of the cognitive science discussion, the brain is the subject. In many places in this chapter I have chosen to use the term "mind/brain" because the distinction between these two entities is difficult to make. For example, the term "brain/mind" is used by authors such as James Ashbrook and Carol Albright, where both may be in view, or both can be seen as one entity.[11] Again, the lines can be blurry.[12]

The mind, in contrast, is the "emergent" part of a person that is his or her personality and thought center.[13] Notably, cognitive science is a science of both the physical and mental. At least in traditional cognitive science, the mind was viewed as a computer, as an information processor.[14] The mind is beyond the brain, the organ, and thus is hard to define in many instances.

In addition, in many academic circles the dualism of mind and body has grown out of favor. Descartes' "substance dualism" states that there are both mental and physical substances.[15] In this study, it is not my objective to defend this type of dualism. At the same time, making distinctions between the emergent self and the physical self can prove useful. In this chapter on cognitive science, the brain and mind will be used separately and intentionally where possible, but where both entities are at work or the lines are blurry, I may refer to mind/brain as previously mentioned.

Evil and the Cognitive Sciences

In speaking of the cognitive sciences, there are many ways that one can discuss the concept of evil as it relates to the brain. There are multiple sciences at work under the one heading of cognitive science. This is just one

11. Ashbrook and Albright, *Humanizing Brain*, 157, for example.

12. Here again are the working definitions of these terms I offered in ch. 1, n. 6:

Brain – The biological organ that is the origin of thought for a person. This term refers only to the biological entity itself.

Mind – The emergent consciousness that arises out of a person's brain. This is where the personality, thought process, etc. are located. It does not have a physical form. When discussing both mind and soul in opposition to body (and brain) some will question whether there is a dualistic nature to humanity. There is still much debate over the idea of emergence in regard to mind.

13. "Emergent" refers to the consciousness that arises out of the biological function of the brain as an organ, as mentioned in the previous footnote.

14. Peterson, *Minding God*, 24–25.

15. Graves, *Mind, Brain*, 3.

reason why it is more useful to speak of the "cognitive sciences" instead of "cognitive science." In this subsection, the focus is on two major categories: how the brain forms myth in order to categorize evil, and how the brain perceives the concept and actions of evil. In the former one sees that creating the category of evil is natural for the mind/brain. In the second, one sees that moral evil can sometimes be a product of a malfunctioning brain or other factors. It is in these two categories that one can connect the work of Evagrius Ponticus and Paul Ricoeur to a discussion with modern cognitive science.

How the Mind Forms Myths of Evil

As Mary Midgley defines them, myths are "imaginative patterns, networks of powerful symbols that suggest particular ways of interpreting the world. They shape its meaning."[16] Thus myth is a combination of interpretations that are used to understand the world that humanity encounters. The first step in understanding evil within the cognitive sciences is to observe how the mind/brain formulates myth.

First, it may be helpful to visit the work of Eugene d'Aquili and Andrew Newberg to discuss their system of "operators." They propose that the brain has specific components that work as a part of the mind. They work like mathematical operators, but are more complex. There are seven such operators: holistic, reductionist, causal, abstractive, binary, quantitative, and the emotional value operator.[17] For purposes of this study, I will focus on the binary operator. The binary operator, they propose, allows the brain to perceive things in terms of "dyads." They list the examples of "good and evil, right and wrong, justice and injustice, happy and sad, and heaven and hell." These pairs obtain meaning in the contrast. Physical particles that are negatively and positively charged are given as an example of how this meaning is only obtained in relation to the other part of the pair. Therefore, "a particle is positive only if it is not negative" and it is negative if it is not positive.[18]

---

16. Midgley, "How Myths Work," 28.

17. d'Aquili and Newberg, *Mystical Mind*, 50–52.

18. Ibid., 55, including quotations following preceding note. There is a flaw in this manner of thinking, however, because particles may also be neutrally charged. Their point is taken, however, and their pairs find meaning in conjunction with each other, noting that the analogy is not always true.

Moving forward, d'Aquili and Newberg state that this operator is specifically relevant to the formation of myth. They note, the "dynamics of myth almost always involve the resolution of whatever opposites comprise the myth structure." For these authors, binary pairs help humans explain "why good things happen to bad people" and vice versa.[19] It is evident from this description that myth is important to the mind's ability to create order, and understanding evil is a key component of myth formation. Showing the importance of myth to their system, in both *The Mystical Mind* and *Why God Won't Go Away* the authors devote the fourth chapter to myth formation.

Myth formation is important to the mind because, as the authors state, drawing on Joseph Campbell, "Myths . . . show us how to be human" and religions are based on myth.[20] They go on to say, "Virtually all myths can be reduced to the same consistent pattern: identify a crucial existential concern, frame it as a pair of incompatible opposites, then find a resolution that alleviates anxiety and allows us to live more happily in the world."[21] Myth functions as a way of combating anxiety, and hence can work as an explanation for the presence of evil. Again drawing on Campbell, they argue that similar myths are found in different cultures. There is a recurrence of myths such as that of a virgin birth or the resurrection of a dead hero. They give a nod to the possibility that this can be partially explained by the sharing of myth between cultures, but also put forth Carl Jung's belief "that myths were the symbolic expression of archetypal ideas."[22]

The brain's perception of reality is described by some basic "cognitive structures," which help in myth formation. There are judgments assigned to certain relationships, for example: "above-below, left-right, in front-behind," etc. "Good" is usually assigned to above, right, and in front, while "bad" is assigned to below, left, and back. These are found to be very common, and possibly universal.[23] Newberg and d'Aquili go on to state that there are three classifications of relationships: affective, spatial, and temporal. They argue for evolutionary bases for these relationships, and these work together to "most probably form the basis of myth

19. Ibid.
20. d'Aquili, Newberg, and Rause, *Why God Won't Go Away*, 55, 56.
21. Ibid., 62.
22. Ibid., 74–75, quotation on 75.
23. d'Aquili and Newberg, *Mystical Mind*, 80–81.

structure."[24] Further, "there is a significant amount of anthropological evidence that the various myths, worldwide, that underlie religions and religious behavior can be grouped into thematic classes." Some argue that the different myths in each of these classes "are transformations of each other" and that ultimately they all represent one deep structure. Newberg and d'Aquili feel that if this is true there must be neuropsychology and neurophysiology undergirding these transformations.[25]

As opposed to those who hold that the "machinery of the brain" inherently relates myth elements dualistically, d'Aquili and Newberg argue that this is more a result of subjectivity that builds on stable relationships that are adaptive as a result of evolution. Therefore the number of transformations is limited by the subset that "contains those transformations that have subjective meaningfulness or, in terms of evolution, have adaptive properties and represent a high degree of isomorphism with the external world."[26] For purposes of the study on evil, whether one holds that we are hardwired to create myth from dyads or that this is a result of what is evolutionarily expedient, i.e., what has worked for survival, there is definite evidence to show that dyadic pairs are used by the mind (and brain) to create myths of evil. Therefore the determination of good and evil is biologically a part of what human beings perceive and know. As d'Aquili and Newberg put it, "Any given surface structure of relationships among elements of a semantic field such as a myth is present and stable simply because it is adaptive psychophysiologically for an individual or social group." They go on to discuss the stability needed for an organism to exist, as "existence itself is defined by a certain degree of permanence." There is always need of adaptation in a changing world, and the environment determines "which surface manifestation of a deep structure will survive . . ."[27] In other words, humans must have a definite system with which to perceive the world as it changes. Myth is formed through this system of dyads that have their roots in evolutionary adaptation. According to this system of evolutionary development, evil is a necessary concept for the survival of the human race. Thus evil is a real concept for the mind to comprehend.

24. Ibid., 81.

25. Ibid., 82, including quotations following preceding note.

26. Ibid., 83–84, quotations on 83 and 84, respectively.

27. Ibid., 84, including quotations following preceding note.

Newberg and d'Aquili go on to state that myth can be resolved both cognitively and ritually. The ritual solution is the most powerful one.[28] There is something about repetitions involved in ritual that cause stimulation in the limbic system in the brain. There is research that shows that "repetitive auditory and visual stimuli can . . . produce an intensely pleasurable, ineffable experience in humans."[29] In addition, ritual can have a secondary effect of curbing aggression in an individual.[30] This may prove beneficial in understanding how Evagrius' cosmological structure and the place of prayer has a practical, beneficial effect on quelling the demons of thought, especially that of anger. Ultimately d'Aquili and Newberg come to the conclusion that ritual alleviates "our existential anxiety" and "allows individual humans to become incorporated into myth and, conversely, allows for the very incarnation of myth."[31] Thus for these authors, speaking from an evolutionary adaptive stance, myth is a key part of how the brain deals with the very anxieties of survival.

In addition, the work of Michael Persinger also argues that the experience of God is a biological phenomenon. Persinger argues that "[t]he God experience has had survival value."[32] He presents two possibilities for belief in God: either it is through faith or through "biochemical systems that display behavior patterns."[33] He argues for the latter and against the dangers of the former.[34] Why is this relevant? Although this is not what d'Aquili and Newberg argue for, it is relevant to a discussion of myth formation as it relates to evil. For purposes of this study, it supports the argument that even from a viewpoint that does not presuppose the existence of God, there is a benefit to be gained from believing in a Deity. This has applications for how a person experiences evil. As with d'Aquili and Newberg, he raises the point of how existential anxiety affects humans, including anxiety causing the deterioration of a person's health.[35] This is relevant for the next subsection.

28. Ibid., 85–86.

29. Ibid., 89.

30. Ibid., 91.

31. Ibid., 93.

32. Persinger, *Neuropsychological Bases of God Beliefs*, 138.

33. Ibid., 144.

34. Ibid., 144–45.

35. Ibid., 148–56, specifically 151.

How the Brain Experiences Evil

Moving away from a discussion of myth, it is now useful to see how the brain (and mind) perceive and experience evil. As just mentioned, "evil" can be experienced in the existential anxiety that causes illness. Continuing from the previous section, Persinger states that anxiety can cause illness such as ulcers and headaches, and even more dire consequences such as cancer.[36] The question that proceeds, "Is illness evil?" or "Is anxiety evil?" I will sidestep a bit, but most would agree that illness can be tragic, and anxiety can lead to evil consequences. As James Ashbrook and Carol Albright present in their book *The Humanizing Brain*, anxiety can lead to "[m]alicious behavior" arising "out of a misguided effort at self-preservation."[37] Thus anxiety has both behavioral and biological consequences. A malfunctioning brain or a mind unable to deal with its own finitude causes people to act out in ways that are evil. I want to be clear, however, that although there are natural, scientific explanations for evil action, this does not release the individual of total responsibility. This is a deeper discussion than can be presented in this study, but let me state that even though sin and evil are a part of the human condition, some humans act differently than others, meaning there is room for responsibility for our actions. In other words, even in the face of a malfunctioning brain, there is room for free will. We are not determined to commit evil in the face of every choice we are given.[38]

Continuing with Ashbrook and Albright, they raise the question of whether sin and evil began with humanity. As I have done, they defer to one's definition of sin or evil, but they offer a brief discussion. For them, sin is only found in humans, but pain is found elsewhere.[39] They go on to state:

> To function optimally, the brain/mind must constantly perform
> various tasks of balancing and integrating. The various sectors of
> the brain have somewhat different biochemical characteristics . . . .
> Yet they must function together. We submit that, if these systems

36. Ibid., 151.

37. Ashbrook and Albright, *Humanizing Brain*, 158–60, quotation on 160.

38. Here I am addressing moral responsibility in the face of individual questions of morality. The broader question of original sin and whether we are predestined to sin may be left for another day.

39. Ashbrook and Albright, *Humanizing Brain*, 157.

do not work well together, the result is likely to be the behaviors we
have identified as sin![40]

This balance is quite important for their discussion. They cite examples
where only "the reptilian brain is activated," leaving behind reason and
emotion, such as the cases of Hitler's army or urban street gangs, where
the brain is not functioning optimally. They go on to discuss examples
where only the limbic system is active without reason, and where reason
is active without emotion, both missing the mark of proper health. The
balance between emotion and reason is key for the brain to function ef-
ficiently. In addition, hormonal response is a part of survival adaptation,
yet in the modern city, these pressures can cause sickness because these
survival techniques are not needed in the same manner.[41] This point is
important to note in discussing the ancient Greek worldview of Evagrius,
where reason is honored highly above emotion (or passion), and hence
self-control is the ideal.[42]

Referencing to the work of Paul Gilbert, the authors present "The
Defense System" and "The Safety System," which help with stress or
calm, respectively. The defense system allows the brain to react to stress
with fight or flight or similar responses. This system is the one referred
to earlier that can malfunction under extreme anxiety and cause one to
act in ways that could be termed "evil." These actions arise when one is
vulnerable, and this breeds anxiety and then evil behavior.[43] In addition,
the Safety System helps to promote "integration and well-being regardless
of circumstances." It functions to help one look for stabilizing factors in
one's environment. The Safety System promotes social behaviors rather
than individual goals. It is easier to act in an acceptable way when the
Safety System is dominant. Ashbrook and Albright state that these two
systems work on chemical and physical laws in which the "brain-mind"
is rooted.[44] Finally they come to the determination that humans are both

40. Ibid.

41. Ibid., 157–58, quotation on 157.

42. This ancient ideal of the spiritual, the intellect, and reason must be seen in its
context, but is relevant in discussing modern cognitive science in the contrast with ancient philosophy.

43. Ashbrook and Albright, *Humanizing Brain*, 158–61. Section titles begin on 158
and 161, respectively.

44. Ibid., 161–62, including quotations following preceding note. They speak on page
162 of it being easier to act "'good'" "[w]hen the safety system is predominant." There is

a "Bottom-Up" and a "Top-Down" system, where human action is determined not only by neurology but also by personal values. They explain that some people do well in the face of danger or loss, and do not give in to evil.[45] They conclude that "Neuroscience is making clear that our brains are made for meaning and for relatedness." Our biology is made to restore healthy persons, which they correlate with "the goodness of creation in Genesis 1."[46] This parallels the balance a person should exemplify and is evidenced in their view of rationality and emotion. One should not be so reductionistic that the many factors involved in creating actions and beliefs are overlooked.

Furthermore, in Jean-Pierre Changeux and Paul Ricoeur's book *What Makes Us Think?* there is a short dialogue between the two authors regarding the nature of evil, which raises some salient points. Changeux begins with a disavowal of the Calvinist worldview that sees suffering as predestined. This is followed by Ricoeur's agreement that humans should not accept evil as punishment from God, stressing his wish not to be associated with the friends of Job, who said that Job received what he deserved. Ricoeur states, "For me, evil is the capacity to challenge the value of life."[47] Changeux replies by drawing on Eugen Drewerman, who "described evil as any force destructive of the community, including sadness, anguish, and despair."[48] He goes on to ponder whether evil is that which is counter to the good of society, replaced by the importance of "the survival of the individual." Ricoeur concurs with this point, believing that even "[t]he word *survival* is very selfish."[49] Before moving forward, I think it important to note Changeux's mention of sadness as evil, which reminds us of Evagrius' demonic thought of sadness. Although his definition may be different than Evagrius', sadness is an important evil that one must be wary of, whether this be in depression or otherwise. Both restlessness and depression often have negative connotations. It is interesting that in

---

not a large amount of space devoted to their discussion, but it is relevant to this study as the brain is shown to be a balance of physical processes that affect what might be termed "evil" behavior. Also notable is their use of "brain-mind" as a term referring to the biological and beyond.

45. Ibid., 162.

46. Ibid., 163.

47. Changeux and Ricoeur, *What Makes Us Think?*, 279–80, quotation on 280.

48. Ibid., 280.

49. Ibid., 281.

Gregory's seven deadly sins, sadness is not among them, but is instead replaced by envy.[50]

Moving on, Changeux connects the concept of fear with that of evil. He states that fear helps humans avoid danger, and so it helps them survive, but it can also cause one to leave the social community, and thus be connected to evil, as he earlier defined it.[51] Ricoeur counters with a three-level analysis of evil. First, that of "description," second, that of "[p]urposeful violence," and third, "a call for help" in preserving "the tradition of goodness."[52] Changeux has a somewhat different opinion on this matter, feeling that where Ricoeur sees this concern for goodness as religion, Changeux sees it not as religion, but as a "common concern as human beings."[53] He also differentiates between the "*cruelty*" of humans and the "ferocity" of animals, stating that only humans can be cruel, something with which Ricoeur agrees, calling animals at most "fierce."[54] This is important due to the nature of human consciousness. Because animals are not conscious of the "suffering that they can inflict upon others" they are not cruel.[55] Thus, in this definition of evil, consciousness of the results of one's actions must be taken into account.

Ultimately, Changeux presents a naturalistic worldview in which morality is not necessarily reliant upon religion, while Ricoeur sees the salvific importance in a definition of evil shown in his use of religion.[56] This is further shown as Ricoeur tries to adopt Paul Tillich's definition that "religion is 'the courage to be.'" Changeux sees this "courage to be" as something humans have innately in their brain, and thus for him Ricoeur provides too exclusive a definition for the term "religion." He sees no need for an "appeal to a higher authority."[57] This discussion goes on, but the important points can be gleaned from what has been stated above. Ricoeur and Changeux agree on many things, but the need for God is not necessarily one of them. For purposes of this study on Evagrius and cognitive

50. Again, for a brief discussion on envy see Newhauser, "Introduction," 4. He also mentions how Gregory drew on the eight thoughts of Evagrius.

51. Changeux and Ricoeur, *What Makes Us Think?*, 281–83.

52. Ibid., 283–85.

53. Ibid., 285.

54. Ibid,. 284.

55. Ibid.

56. Ibid., 285.

57. Ibid., 286, including quotations following preceding note.

science, evil can be seen in the mind/brain as a result of divine action or a natural, evolutionary development. It can also be seen as both.

Clearly the natural worldview still lends itself to the questions of how "evil" occurs. In Ashbrook and Albright we see the need for a balanced mind/brain. When one survival system is emphasized too much, it causes malfunction. Their work is especially important in raising the question of how some people overcome evil despite biology. For them both biology and values are important, so clearly both values and personal freedom are a part of what decides whether one gives in to moral evil.[58] Persinger sees belief in God as helpful, but solely because of evolutionary reasons.[59] So it is clear that the mind/brain is a key battleground for evil in that it is the originator of many evils, whether this source is initially supernatural, natural, or somehow emergent.

Prayer, Cognitive Science, and Psychotherapy

Moving away from a direct discussion of evil and the cognitive sciences, it is now necessary to discuss how prayer and psychotherapy affect the brain/mind. Here is an opening for us to connect the ideas on evil and the thoughts with Evagrius' remedies of prayer and spiritual disciplines. In this manner the cognitive science discussion will parallel Evagrius' cosmology.[60] By showing some of the work of cognitive science in both the creation of evil and the way spirituality affects the brain, one can see Evagrius' system as it relates to these areas of cognitive science. Both the brain scan work of d'Aquili and Newberg and the "spiritually integrated psychotherapy" of Kenneth Pargament will provide useful discussion, as well as a broader discussion about prayer.

Brain Scans: d'Aquili and Newberg

Returning to the work of Eugene d'Aquili and Andrew Newberg (with Vince Rause), research is presented that may show that "mystical experience is biologically, observably, and scientifically real."[61] Before addressing

58. Again, this is noted in Ashbrook and Albright , *Humanizing Brain*, 162–63.

59. This is discussed just prior to this subsection in the heading on myth and evil.

60. Evagrius' cosmology here refers to his view on the universe's hierarchy. For him, material things are below immaterial things, which are below God.

61. d'Aquili, Newberg, and Rause, *Why God Won't Go Away*, 7.

such a large claim, it is first necessary to present highlights of their research and its importance for this study.

In *Why God Won't Go Away*, the authors explain how they ran tests on Tibetan monks and Franciscan nuns as they went into meditative states in order to observe these mystical states. The first few pages of the text describe how Robert, a Buddhist monk, went through the testing process.[62] He was to meditate, and when getting close to the peak of his meditation, he was to tug on a piece of twine that was attached to Andrew Newberg's finger in the other room. That way d'Aquili and Newberg would know at what point he reached the meditative peak, which is what they were most interested in observing.[63] At the point of this peak, when the twine is pulled, a radioactive substance is injected into Robert's vein and he is then taken into a room where a SPECT camera—single photon emission computed tomography—scans his head and shows how the subject's brain looked just after injection, when he was reaching his meditative peak.[64] What it showed is that before the process, his brain was very active and the scans showed red and yellow all around, but when he reached the peak of meditation, there were blues and greens in what they call the OAA—orientation association area—showing reduced neurological activity.[65] The OAA is the area of the brain that is responsible for orienting oneself "in physical space—it keeps track of which end is up, helps us judge angles and distances, and allows us to negotiate safely the dangerous physical landscape around us."[66] This is notable for their study as for this one because of how meditation has been described by the monks as well as the nuns that were tested.[67] Robert described the approach to his spiritually meditative peak thus:

> First, he says, his conscious mind quiets, allowing a deeper, simpler part of himself to emerge. Robert believes that this inner self is the truest part of who he is, the part that never changes. For Robert, this inner self is not a metaphor or an attitude; it is literal, constant, and real. It is what remains when worries, fears, desires, and all other preoccupations of the conscious mind are stripped

62. Ibid., 1–7.

63. Ibid., 1.

64. Ibid., 3.

65. Ibid., 4, 5–6.

66. Ibid., 4–5, including quotation.

67. Ibid., 2, 7.

away. He considers this inner self the very essence of his being. If pressed, he might even call it his soul.

Whatever Robert calls this deeper consciousness, he claims that when it emerges during those moments of meditation when he is most completely absorbed in looking inward, he suddenly understands that his inner self is not an isolated entity, but that he is inextricably connected to all of creation.[68]

The Franciscan nuns who underwent the same testing showed similar results, but added in their description that at the peak of meditation they felt "a tangible sense of the closeness of God and a mingling with Him." Newberg and d'Aquili relate this to the past voice of Angela of Foligno, also a Franciscan nun.[69] These accounts as they relate to the results of the scan are important to note. The tangible evidence of a change in a person's spatial center in the brain seems to make logical sense in connection with the feeling of being close to God or creation because the boundaries of space are no longer felt. Hence the person meditating feels at one with everything because of the meditation's effect on the orientation association area, which creates how one views his or her own physical boundaries.[70]

The account of Robert and the mention of the nuns are important for our study of Evagrius also. For now, let us discuss this only briefly, but the testimony of the subjects of d'Aquili and Newberg's testing shows something about the nature of this sort of deep meditation and its bringing oneself closer to God. When one goes inward like this, one can feel closer to God—or nature, as the Buddhist might describe it. The worries that Robert describes as leaving behind sound like the thoughts that Evagrius describes overcoming. The closeness to God that the nuns describe sounds similar to the place of God that is the result of pure prayer.

Ultimately, Newberg and d'Aquili use this research to propose a state of mind that they refer to as "absolute unitary being" (AUB for short). Although it is difficult to achieve this ultimate state, the brain can achieve mystical states that are less than AUB and still be "in spiritual states of inexpressible power and sublimity."[71] This is important in relation to Evagrius, because mystical states are shown to move along a continuum, just as in Evagrius' writings the path to pure prayer is full of different steps

68. Ibid., 2.

69. Ibid., 7, including quotation.

70. Ibid., 4–5.

71. Ibid., 123.

of prayer and spiritual disciplines. AUB "is a state in which the subject loses all awareness of discrete limited being and of the passage of time, and even experiences an obliteration of the self-other dichotomy."[72] In contrast, mystical states that do not reach this state they entitle "Lesser Mystical States." These states they describe as most likely "mild to moderate stimulation of certain neuronal circuits (of the lateral hypothalamus) that generate a mild to moderate fear accompanied by a sense of exaltation."[73] These states are key for both this study and d'Aquili and Newberg's for they present a contrast to AUB and a peak state of meditation. Religious experiences of this sort can be created by meditation, ritual, or even spontaneously.[74] Interestingly, when these lesser states are engaged, they prevent AUB from being obtained. Only a partial change will happen, not a full one: "One or the other [side] might be totally deafferented, but neither will be totally deafferented at the same time."[75] Again this helps to support how general religious experience is observed in the brain, and enforces the different brain movements depending on the level of spiritual effect. It also shows AUB to be a unique event in itself. For further study, there are many texts that discuss religious experience and ritual, but due to space I will not address them in this book.[76]

The authors go on to discuss AUB in relation to some of the operators that they previously presented.[77] In addition to the binary operator that was previously mentioned, the holistic operator is also significant. They state that for theologians the concept of AUB must be connected with the foundational myth, which is defined as "the primary myth on which the religion is based."[78] It is obvious to the study of Evagrius that the Christian

72. d'Aquili and Newberg, *Mystical Mind*, 109–10.

73. Ibid., 102.

74. Ibid., 103.

75. Ibid., 117–18, quotation on 117. On 41 the authors describe deafferentation: "In deafferentation incoming information (or afferents) into a brain structure are 'cut off.' This cutting off is an actual physiological process, which may be partial or total." On 42 they go on to state: "If deafferentation of a structure occurs to a significant degree, the neurons within that structure are no longer under the influence of any other parts of the brain and they begin to fire on their own."

76. One text that addresses ritual is McCauley and Lawson, *Bringing Ritual to Mind*. Another excellent general text on cognitive science is Peterson, *Minding God*, which contains a section on religious experience on 99–117.

77. d'Aquili and Newberg, *Mystical Mind*, 163–76.

78. Ibid., 167, 7, quotation on 7.

theologian is limited, at least in some respects, by the confessional nature of historic Christianity. The authors state that they are focusing more on universal questions, but do raise this point to the reader. Within the discussion of a holistic operator they also raise the question of whether "lesser unitary states" can be exclusive. They believe the answer is yes, at least the ones closest to AUB, based on their neuropsychological analysis. Thus a lesser state could be exclusively Christian, Hindu, or Muslim, but AUB could not.[79] Again, this may be useful in looking at the continuum of Evagrius' thought.

Overall, d'Aquili and Newberg's work shows that there is at least a possible correlation between the science of the brain and mystical experiences. Their work has a direct connection to the work of Evagrius if one is looking for scientific explanations of Evagrius' mystical descriptions, which is part of the goal of this book. Notably, the state of AUB is described by most as "pure consciousness." It is definitely "not local consciousness or subjective awareness."[80] Is this the state of pure prayer that Evagrius described? There is no way of actually knowing without doing empirical testing on Evagrius, or perhaps testing a monk who follows the Evagrian process, but there is definitely room for dialogue.

The work of d'Aquili and Newberg, however, is not without its critique. Anne Runehov has recently done an evaluation of their work followed by some important discussion.[81] To begin, she presents a few suggestions that would have made their testing stronger. First, the testing group was rather small and consisted of Buddhists and Christians who had been meditating regularly for at least fifteen years. If they are making a universal claim about religious experience, it may have been helpful to add other perspectives, for example, of Muslims and Hindus. It also may have helped to have varying ages of men and women participating in the study, as everyone was between the ages of thirty-eight and fifty-two.[82] Second, she suggests that for the control group of non-meditators, it would have been helpful to have them "concentrate on a poem" or something similar, and she relates this to the work of Nina Azari and her experiments on religious experience. She had one group memorize a

79. Ibid., 167–68. Both a discussion of myth and lesser states are contained in this section on the holistic operator.

80. Ibid., 201.

81. Runehov, *Sacred or Neural?*, specifically ch. 6.

82. Ibid., 174–75.

psalm from the Bible, while another group memorized a poem, and later both groups underwent a PET scan.[83] Thus Azari's work has parallels with the work of d'Aquili and Newberg, and they might have strengthened their testing in this way. Third, Runehov suggests differentiating types of meditation in the image scanning. This would allow for different types of scans. For example, in looking at the via negativa or the via positiva forms of mediation, one could see how they differently affect the brain.[84]

Further, Runehov raises the question of whether there is an "Invariant Element across the Religions?"[85] This is somewhat irrelevant to this particular study of Evagrius, as I do not intend to look for a universal mystical experience, but the work of d'Aquili and Newberg does raise this possibility. That said, this is an important critique of their research because it does tend toward a reductionistic approach to religion in the cognitive sciences. She raises a similar question in asking if all neural experiences are equal.[86] To this she states that some neuroscientists argue that brains are unique, like faces. Moreover, on a neurological level, the way in which one person experiences something may not be the same as another. The example of eating a piece of apple pie is used. One person might be hungry while eating it, while another is not. One may find it sweeter than another. These examples draw on "*the multiple realization principle*" that "dictates that even if we do the same things, we will still have different neural values." So it is possible that two people meditate but have different brain pathways engaged in reaching the supposed AUB.[87]

In addition, Runehov asks if AUB actually exists. In answer to this she raises the relevant point that AUB cannot be proven because in order to do this, philosophically one must prove that God or an Ultimate Reality exists.[88] Another question raised is how one experiences "an experience without an object." In the end, "what is seen on the computer screen of the SPECT does not refer to God or Ultimate Reality but to neural activity."[89] These are good scientific questions to ask, and this broaches the question

83. Ibid., 175–76.

84. Ibid., 176.

85. Ibid., 178–86, title on 178.

86. Ibid., 186–88.

87. Ibid., 186–87, quotations on 187.

88. Ibid., 188.

89. Ibid., 191.

of how their data is being interpreted. I would argue that it does not create absolute proof of a religious experience, but it does tend toward that possibility. Specifically, it can help give some insight into historic mystical experiences, which is, in part, what this study is attempting to do. This is especially helpful because the meditative experiences of the subjects of d'Aquili and Newberg's experiments are rooted in deep spiritual tradition themselves.

Due to space concerns, let me close this discussion of Runehov's work with a relevant point about thalamic values. Newberg and d'Aquili claim "the meditators had a significantly different thalamic laterality index at baseline compared to the control group of non-meditators." She questions the reason for this. Was it because of the long practice of meditation, a physiological difference at birth, or a developed talent? She addresses the problems with each solution, feeling the latter is the "most rational" choice.[90] This raises a question for the study of Evagrius and the physical brain: Does the exercise of the practices and prayer cause this biological change in a person, allowing them to reach the state of pure prayer (or AUB)? Can someone build up this ability? There is more to Runehov's discussion, but this question is relevant for this study of Evagrius because it may show that Evagrius' system of reaching pure prayer can strengthen an inherent ability or create the ability where there was none.

Clearly the research of d'Aquili and Newberg is limited, and has room for improvement that perhaps will happen in subsequent years. They present a contrast to the work of Persinger in that they see religious experience as more than just brain activity. They give credence to the testimony of their subjects' experiences, pointing beyond mere neurons.[91] They do not reach total proof of their models through their experiments, and cannot prove that there is only one AUB (which does not necessarily hurt our study of Evagrius specifically), but there is much to gain from the work they have done.[92] Runehov has raised some important questions about their work, and in more detailed ways than this study of Evagrius allows us to investigate. The questions this raises from an empirical testing perspective are clearly relevant for a look at Evagrius' cosmology. In addition there is research in psychotherapy that is also pertinent to his worldview.

90. Ibid., 192–93, quotation on 192.

91. Ibid., 200.

92. Ibid., 199.

Spiritually Integrated Psychotherapy: Kenneth Pargament[93]

There has been quite a bit of recent work in the field of religion and spirituality as it relates to psychotherapy, and the work of Kenneth Pargament represents some of the strongest in this field. It is also seen in centers such as the Center for the Study of Health, Religion, and Spirituality at Indiana State University.[94] In general, however, psychological research in regard to physical and mental health has neglected religion and spirituality factors. Although this is disappointing, there is some research available. In fact, "there is evidence that religion and spirituality are distinctive dimensions that add unique explanatory power to the prediction of physical and mental health."[95] Spirituality is an important component in the physical and mental well-being of some subjects, and this is beginning to be shown in psychological research. There are different ways that religion and spirituality can contribute to a person's health, from attributing the sacred to certain aspects of life, either physically or psychologically, to giving people "a sense of their ultimate destinations in life." Notable for this study is not only this sense of destination, but "viable pathways for reaching these destinations."[96] In relation to this, Kenneth Pargament and Peter Hill state:

> Similarly, in the pursuit of spiritual growth or a relationship with the transcendent, the individual may be more likely to avoid the vices (e.g., gluttony, lust, envy, pride) and practice the virtues (e.g., compassion, forgiveness, gratitude, hope) that have themselves been associated with mental and physical health status.[97]

In various studies "higher levels of an intrinsic religious orientation have been associated with better mental health . . ."[98] This reduction in vice as well as the increase of religion and spirituality has a direct empirical correlation to the eight thoughts of Evagrius.

In addition, Pargament makes the case that "spiritually integrated therapy is not simply one more set of techniques that can be piggybacked

---

93. This term comes from Pargament, *Spiritually Integrated Psychotherapy*.

94. More information about the center can be found at their Web site: http://www.indstate.edu/psychology/cshrs.htm.

95. Hill and Pargament, "Advances in Conceptualization," 71–72, quotation on 72.

96. Ibid., 68.

97. Ibid.

98. Ibid.

onto other therapies. It grows out of a different way of thinking about problems, solutions, and human nature more generally."[99] This way of therapy draws on both theory and research. It is both "a systematic way of thinking about spirituality" and also rooted in empirical research. To the extent that empirical research is available, Pargament draws from it.[100] The research so far is limited, but it is hopeful and indicates that SIP (spiritually integrated psychotherapy) is a beneficial approach to treatment.[101]

For purposes of this study on Evagrius and cognitive science, the empirical nature of this method of therapy is most important. For thousands of years, prayer as part of a spiritual worldview has been accepted by many as an approach to combating illness, mental or otherwise. It is in dialogue with science that this acceptance must be tempered with empirical results. Along these lines, some research does show that SIP does work. There are studies from the early 1980s that show SIP works better than no therapy at all, which should make sense.[102] However, Pargament takes this a step further to ask if SIP is more effective than other types of treatment. Some earlier studies show that there is "no difference in the effectiveness of 'religion-accommodative' cognitive-behavioral treatments and standard cognitive-behavioral therapies for Christian clients with depression."[103] However there are other studies that do show better results for a spiritual approach. Many of these studies are from the last several years. One example is that of Amy Wachholtz, who "found that spiritual meditation was superior to secular meditation and progressive relaxation for college students with vascular headaches."[104] Although the research is still far from complete, the results are positive up until now. Pargament raises two points in regard to the research. One, even in comparing secular and spiritual treatments, it might be impossible to separate the two. Two, SIP, even if not more effective than other treatment, is not less effective.[105] Other research covered treatments ranging from those

99. Pargament, *Spiritually Integrated Psychotherapy*, 199–200.

100. Ibid., 19–20.

101. Ibid., 320.

102. Ibid., 325–26.

103. Ibid., 326.

104. Ibid., 326–27, quotation on 326.

105. Ibid., 327–28. The first point is also brought out in an example by Pargament on 14–15, where even those in a secular group of treatment used prayer in an experiment regarding forgiveness.

with depression and schizophrenia to those wanting to forgive more, and thus did not necessarily engage prayer and the "demonic."[106] However, psychotherapy strives to heal a person's psyche, and the research seems to present an empirical link between the spiritual and the scientific in regard to treatment, i.e., research shows that spiritual therapy is superior to therapy without the spiritual component.

Pargament speaks from a Jewish perspective and admittedly presents a Western monotheistic bias. His approach, however, is ideally pluralistic and he seems to strive for this ideal.[107] In engaging Evagrius, this bias is not harmful, but in looking to expand the discussion, pluralistic viewpoints may have to be considered even further. I have chosen not to burden the reader with the details of implementing SIP, as they are not crucial to this study, but this is clearly a part of psychological research that will become more and more important to devote research time to investigate. Early indications are that adding a spiritual component to therapy only benefits the treatment, showing that pious approaches to a person's health and battling "evil" may be vindicated by empirical method.[108]

Discussion of Morality and Evil in Cognitive Science

In summary, this chapter has addressed the mind/brain distinction and William James, the way the mind/brain formulates myth and experiences evil, and the way the brain reacts to forms of spirituality, both biologically and psychologically. William James presents ideas relevant to cognitive science that give current-day readers an early view of questions for the cognitive sciences. His definitions and thoughts are useful for connecting the age of Darwin with current research. In addition, the mind/brain

106. Ibid., 326–27.

107. Ibid., 20–21, 305.

108. I think it important to note that lack of empirical proof of the effectiveness of spirituality does not make it any less beneficial, and empirical testing only provides a limited truth based upon the method itself. In gaining credibility among modern science, however, this empirical evidence will help to build dialogue between spirituality and the sciences.

Also important to note is that there are other recent studies showing the connection between the spiritual and treatment. In a recent paper under review, "God Give Me Strength," Bennett and Elliott explore the connection between prayer and other forms of self-disclosure. For them, prayer works "as self-disclosure to God and can provide for similar health benefits" (35–36, quotation on 36).

distinction is also important as one observes the findings of the cognitive sciences and converses with Evagrius Ponticus.

Second, the brain naturally lends itself to the formation of myth. This is shown in philosophy through the work of Paul Ricoeur and in cognitive science through the work of d'Aquili and Newberg. Even the work of Michael Persinger would support this conclusion. The research of these scholars upholds the notion that human beings define evil using biological, cognitive structures that are a part of their persons. This could be argued in different ways: that humans define evil where there is no evil to make order out of things, or that evil does indeed exist and human mechanism is available to properly define it. This also lays groundwork for moral responsibility. The human brain can malfunction in the pursuit of survival and cause a person to commit evil acts. But is this truly a malfunction? In the sense of ideal brain operation, yes. On the other hand, because it is so much a part of human action, it also can be seen as a part of normal, though not ideal brain function, leaving open the debate over sin and whether it is a biological taint.

Lastly, the discussion on AUB and SIP presents research that shows incipient, empirical evidence that the brain is geared for spirituality. The brain scans of d'Aquili and Newberg seem to show that at the moment of the peak of meditation, a person can become unaware of spatial boundaries, thus mimicking a feeling of closeness with God or the universe (or is this actual closeness?).[109] The work of Kenneth Pargament shows that adding a spiritual dimension in psychotherapy may be more useful than regular methods alone. If true, it would tend to enforce the viewpoint that moral evil and the "evil" of mental malfunction can be treated by spiritual means, at least in part.

As a brief note, another area of research that is growing and may support the Evagrian—and more generally monastic—worldview is that of finding moral exemplars. Moral exemplars are people that embody moral actions in a way beyond the average person. There is research currently being done by scholars such as Michael Spezio and Gregory Peterson showing that people learn morality by imitating moral exemplars. This would seem to support the notion that learning is done first by imitating

109. I would argue that this very well could be actual closeness to God, but want to be careful on two fronts: one, I do not necessarily want to attribute divine experience wholly to a biologically observable event, and two, it could be that this is only showing us part of the experience.

actions.[110] If true, this would indicate that the way to become a moral exemplar is to imitate one, and thus Evagrius' system of spiritual practices preceding the levels of prayer would be the first step in becoming more moral. More virtue may lead to more stability of character.[111] Thus the virtues of Evagrius' system may empirically support stability of character.

If the growing research points toward spirituality being empirically viable for mental health and the reduction of evil, this opens a possible dialogue between Evagrius' beliefs with the cognitive science of the twenty-first century. Now that this dialogue has been shown to be possible, we can move to the final chapter in order to synthesize this work and construct ideas about evil and how to battle it.

110. Peterson, Spezio, and Van Slyke. Presentation at the American Academy of Religion 2008 Annual Meeting.

111. Ibid. This comment was made during the question-and-answer session.

five

A Synthesis of Evagrius
and Cognitive Science

Constructing a View of Evil

T HIS STUDY HAS TAKEN us on a journey though aspects of theology, philosophy, history, and science. But at the end of this presentation, what have we learned, and how is this applicable? I have attempted to speak predominately to the Christian, who, despite his confessional and devout belief in the foundations of Christianity, still harbors doubt as to whether there is merit to the prayer life and supernatural language of demons. I also address the person who may have doubt about the reality of mystic experiences, yet feels her faith says that there is basis to these experiences. Many believers have some degree of scientific training and, as a result, see science as such a final arbiter of truth that it makes their faith difficult. In mainline Protestant denominations, mysticism is looked at very skeptically, and with good reason. The Enlightenment standards of truth cause us to be wary of those who claim direct experience with God. It is with this same wariness that we approach talk of the devil, demons, and other "supernatural" language, despite the fact that Christianity is based in the supernatural act of a God-man who was resurrected from the dead.

The main focus of this study has been on bringing Evagrius' writings on evil and prayer into a dialogue with current cognitive science. This is done in order to better understand his writings and to see that they have merit for the present-day Christian who struggles with anxiety and moral evil, whether they want to attribute this to demons, original sin, or a broader human condition. It is my desire that this book has helped to present some empirical backing and hope to those who wish to understand their own spiritual life better. Anxiety and moral evil are difficulties of the Christian life, and prayer and Scripture are, as they have always been, two of the greatest tools to combat these obstacles to spiritual health.

In this final chapter, I present individual syntheses between the previous three chapters, allowing connections to be made between these disparate disciplines. The eight thoughts of Evagrius open a discussion on moral evil from a supernatural, patristic perspective. Comparing this with the symbolic myth work of Paul Ricoeur and the scientific perspective of cognitive science allows us to construct a viewpoint that gives ancient Christian perspectives on evil and humanity a place for dialogue in the scientific realm. This has both a theoretical and a practical component, as is witnessed in the work of Evagrius in the patristic world, and d'Aquili and Newberg, Ricoeur and Changeux, and Kenneth Pargament in the present day.

In order to construct this theological perspective, one must engage the previous three chapters in a dialogical way. First, a modern look at Eastern Orthodox views of psychotherapy benefits the engagement of these topics. Orthodoxy has much to say about the human mind, and a cursory overview of some relevant themes is useful. Second, this must be followed by a synthesis of the study up to this juncture. Seeing the connections between Evagrius, Ricoeur, and cognitive science allows for the constructive engagement that will follow. Last, a constructive, dialogical discussion presents a view of moral evil, as it relates to this study, that is both theoretically and practically tenable.

Orthodox Psychotherapy

In recent years there have been some writings from the Orthodox community regarding how Orthodox spiritual practices relate to modern psychotherapy. Because this is directly relevant for an application of Evagrius' methods to the cognitive sciences, including psychotherapy, this discussion is especially pertinent. From at least one Orthodox perspective the priest works predominately as a therapist in his role as a confessor.[1] As Metropolitan Hierotheos Vlachos describes it, therapy in regard to the soul is a "freeing of the nous." Due to humanity being "sick" because of its fall from God, the nous must be restored from captivity.[2] From this viewpoint, the Orthodox priest is specially equipped to administer this therapy. Early on in his argument he states:

> From what has been said so far it is clear that Christianity is prin-
> cipally a science which cures, that is to say, a psychotherapeutic
> method and treatment. The same should be said of theology. It is
> not a philosophy but mainly a therapeutic treatment. Orthodox
> theology shows clearly that on the one hand it is a fruit of therapy
> and on the other hand it points the way to therapy. In other words,
> only those who have been cured and have attained communion
> with God are theologians, and they alone can show Christians the
> true way to reach the 'place' of cure. So theology is both a fruit and
> a method of therapy.[3]

In this lengthy quote are found two major points. First, that Christianity is a "science which cures," and second, only the person who has "been cured" is a theologian, and can be a leader in this health-seeking endeavor to lead others to the "cure." He goes on to present some of the methods for curing the soul. He stresses *right faith*, putting an emphasis on doctrine. One must also *feel ill*. "Self-knowledge is one of the first steps to a cure." If one doesn't know he is sick he cannot get treatment.[4] Notably, Vlachos also points to *asceticism*.[5] He closes this particular chapter by stressing that "Christianity is a therapeutic science." He sees the loss of tradition in the Orthodox Church to be rooted "in the loss of the therapeutic method and of actual therapists."[6]

Another important point evident in Vlachos' presentation, and particularly relevant for this study of Evagrius, is the way he draws from the Orthodox tradition. While not surprising that he draws on this tradition, I want to point out the very conspicuous absence of Evagrius Ponticus. This also is not surprising because Evagrius is viewed as a heretic, but

1. Vlachos, *Orthodox Psychotherapy*, 57.
2. Ibid., 36.
3. Ibid., 30–31.
4. Ibid., 42–43, quotation on 43.
5. Ibid., 47.
6. Ibid., 55.

it raises the importance of his work. The eight thoughts are referenced and called the "eight evil thoughts." However, they are attributed to John Cassian, despite the fact that Cassian transmitted the work of Evagrius to the West.[7] There are two references to Evagrius in the book, but in one instance he is a side note, noting that St. Dorotheos agrees with him. In the other reference, the idea of "cutting off the thoughts" is attributed to Evagrius, but the presentation is brief.[8] Vlachos' work contains a large discussion on the thoughts and passions, yet these two references to Evagrius are all that is to be found, and one of these is made through the work of another scholar.[9]

Vlachos' work is important in two major regards. First, it shows how Orthodoxy can be viewed as therapy, which is relevant for dialogue with the cognitive sciences. Second, he shows the importance of the thoughts and their treatment in the exercise of Orthodox psychotherapy, and as a sub-point, the limited attribution of Evagrius' work to this discussion, despite the centrality of his work to some aspects of Orthodox psychotherapy.

Further, in a more recent work, Archbishop Chrysostomos approaches Orthodox psychotherapy from a point of engagement with modern psychotherapy. He also states that "Orthodox psychotherapy is aimed at the restoration of the soul."[10] He makes a clear distinction between the aims of secular and Orthodox therapies. While psychotherapy heals the ego or self, Orthodox psychotherapy is spiritual and deals with the theological anthropology and soteriology of a person.[11] He is more skeptical of those who apply Orthodox methods as a substitute for conventional psychotherapeutic methods, specifically mentioning Hesychastic methods.[12]

Chrysostomos makes a point to speak out against the trend of connecting spiritual disorders with psychological maladies. An example of

7. Ibid., 289–91, quotation on 289.

8. Ibid., 217, 248. These are the only two times Evagrius is mentioned here according to the index.

9. Ibid., 214–309. Here one can find a lengthy discussion on the thoughts and the passions. Included in this is the treatment of the thoughts and the passions, beginning on 228 and 267, respectively. On 228 he lists the cures of the thoughts as "**watchfulness, attentiveness, hesychia, and cutting off evil thoughts**" (emphasis original).

10. Chrysostomos, *Guide to Orthodox Psychotherapy*, 106.

11. Ibid., 100–101.

12. Ibid., 103.

this is in the use of the term "noonday demon," which, he states, some wrongly equate with clinical depression.[13] As with Vlachos, he neglects Evagrius while quoting John Cassian's reference to Evagrius' "noonday demon" mentioned in the *Praktikos*.[14] Evagrius, in fact, is not mentioned at all in the index to his text.[15] Chrysostomos also alludes to the work of Andrew Solomon, who writes about depression, and finds in Augustine and medieval tradition the roots of the Christian meaning of depression. He states that Solomon's book title, *The Noonday Demon*, comes from John Cassian.[16] In this same book, Solomon references Evagrius briefly, but attributes the title to Cassian, then Evagrius.[17]

In addition, Chrysostomos states that the church fathers "suggest that those who are mentally ill—as well as those who engage in sinful behaviors—are more susceptible to influence from demonic or evil psychic influences of Satanic provenance," but mainly because the illness prevents them from fighting these influences properly.[18] This is an important concept because it relates to the idea of a malfunctioning brain and the body's ability to heal itself. If it cannot do so properly because of mental illness, or sinfulness, this connects the fathers' ideas to those of the cognitive sciences because it shows a link between brain health and spiritual health for the person battling evil thoughts.[19]

Overall, Chrysostomos is presenting a cautious approach to Orthodox psychotherapy in its use in secular psychotherapy. They have different functions, however some aspects of the Orthodox approach may be useful in the secular, especially with Orthodox Christians. It seems his wish is to integrate some aspects of Orthodox psychotherapy with secular psychotherapy, but he wants to be cautious. His caution is important to note for a study such as this one because it challenges the notion of connecting the

13. Ibid., 103–4.

14. Ibid., 104. This reference to Evagrius can be found in *Praktikos* 6.12 (Evagrius, *Evagrius of Pontus*, 99).

15. Chrysostomos, *Guide to Orthodox Psychotherapy*, 127–29.

16. Ibid., 105.

17. Solomon, *Noonday Demon*, 292–93. Solomon may be excused attributing the phrase "noonday demon" predominately to Cassian, if indeed he is tracing the Western use of depression as Chrysostomos states. The fact that he gives nod to Evagrius also shows his awareness of the reference.

18. Chrysostomos, *Guide to Orthodox Psychotherapy*, 105, quotation and paraphrase.

19. Again, a discussion of brain malfunction is found in Ashbrook and Albright, *Humanizing Brain*, 156–63.

patristic tradition with that of secular psychotherapy.[20] Because he does have commitments "to the scientific method in the evaluation of therapeutic modalities," he has credibility in both the scientific and theological realms, which allows his cautions to be taken more seriously within his viewpoint of Orthodox psychotherapy.[21]

In looking at some of the literature on Orthodox psychotherapy, a few things stand out. First, Evagrius is neglected, despite his prominence in the methods employed. This is most likely a symptom of the accepted anathematization of his writings, but raises questions about the use of his work without original attribution.[22] This adds to the importance of this study of Evagrius and cognitive science. Not only is it a relevant theological endeavor, but it also shows the importance of Evagrius' work in dialogue with Orthodox psychotherapy. Second, a distinction must be made about the purpose of Orthodox psychotherapy in conjunction with general psychotherapy. It focuses on a theological anthropology versus a secular biology. However, it is relevant to a discussion of broader psychotherapy, as evidenced in the fact that the American Psychological Association added "a chapter on psychotherapy with Eastern Orthodox Christians" to its *Handbook of Psychotherapy and Religious Diversity* in the year 2000.[23] This emphasizes the differences in the Orthodox approach, while acknowledging its usefulness in psychotherapy. Third, some of the parallels to be drawn from the church fathers and secular psychotherapy are already present in Orthodox psychotherapy, but may be interpreted differently. This is evidenced in the previous discussion, where Chrysostomos speaks against a misunderstanding of the term "noonday demon." This interpretation must be taken into account when drawing parallels, but new viewpoints must also be allowed while trying to avoid anachronistic interpretations—a difficult endeavor when engaging topics more than 1600 years apart. With these points in mind, a greater synthesis of Evagrius and cognitive science can be reached.

20. Chrysostomos, *Guide to Orthodox Psychotherapy*, 108.

21. Ibid., 102.

22. Casiday, "Gabriel Bunge," 249–50. He mentions the anathematization of Evagrius' work.

23. Chrysostomos, *Guide to Orthodox Psychotherapy*, xvii.

Evagrius' Work in Dialogue: Synthesizing Evagrius, Evil, and Cognitive Science

Now that the foundations have been laid for intimate dialogue, it is necessary to compare the major components of this study. This will be done in three sub-sections, placing chapters 2 through 4 in discussion with each other. First, Evagrius' thoughts will be considered with the work of Hadot, Ricoeur, and the broader topic of evil. Second, evil will be considered in conversation with cognitive science. Third, the work of Evagrius will be reflected on in light of cognitive science, completing the cycle of dialogue. Each of these sub-sections summarizes the major points that should be gleaned from this study thus far, setting up a constructive theology to follow.

Evil and Evagrius' Thoughts

Chapter 2 presented the work of Evagrius as it pertains to the eight thoughts. Chapter 3 first described the work of Pierre Hadot in recovering Greek philosophy, in order to interpret Evagrius in context, and later discussed the work of Paul Ricoeur, who presented a background of symbols leading to myth from which evil can be understood in both the fourth century and today. The first step in constructing a theology that encompasses the readings set forth previously must start with this interaction. First, one must view Evagrius' work through that of Hadot. Second, one must read Evagrius with Ricoeur's structure in mind, while also allowing both Evagrius and Ricoeur to dialogue.

By looking at Evagrius through the eyes of Hadot, one sees that Evagrius very much fits into the standard tradition of Greek philosophy. Instead of Hadot's "philosophy as a way of life" perhaps we should say that for Evagrius theology is a way of life. Evagrius' cosmology is the key foundational component to his approach to the thoughts and prayer. This cosmology, as well as the approach itself, is clearly rooted in the Greek philosophers. Evagrius' spiritual exercises as a way of controlling the passions are rooted directly in the Greek philosophical tradition. This also connects back to his place amidst the Egyptian ascetics. His approach is very Greek, which distinguishes him from some of his Egyptian contemporaries. In addition, as stated in chapter 2, he is also drawing on the

Egyptian tradition, making him even more unique.[24] The major points we must gain from a reading of Hadot are that Evagrius is a product of the Greek philosophical tradition and that this is foundational for reading his cosmology as well as approach to the thoughts and prayer.

As regards Ricoeur and Evagrius, there is a parallel movement in Ricoeur's progression of symbols from defilement to sin to guilt, and Evagrius' progression of battling the thoughts moving from spiritual disciplines to contemplation of nature to contemplation of the spiritual to contemplation of God. Both reflect an outward-to-inward movement. The symbolic progression of evil mirrors the practices that overcome that evil in Evagrius. The underlying symbols of evil in Ricoeur's presentation show themselves to be foundationally relevant in Evagrius' work, in the same manner as they are for Christian theology.

In addition, of the four myths of evil that Ricoeur draws from these symbols—the chaotic creation myth, the tragic myth, the Adamic myth, and the myth of the pre-existent soul—few are explicitly relevant in developing Evagrius' discussion on evil, but all are implicitly relevant. The myth of the pre-existent soul is especially important to his work, and not only because of his belief in the pre-existence of the soul. This myth divides humans into a body and a soul and focuses on the soul. It is often combined with the Adamic myth to create a myth of the fall.[25] In addition, all anthropological dualism tries to rationalize this myth.[26] It is for this very reason that this myth, in addition to the Adamic myth, is relevant to many, if not most historical studies of Christian theology and evil.

Furthermore, in Evagrius' work this dualism is clearly apparent, as the body is involved in the initial stages of defeating moral evil, but not so much the later states. The Greek ideal of the intellect over the body is the foundation upon which his program of prayer is based. Ricoeur's conception of the foundations of evil are clear in Evagrius' thought, as all four myths compose the tradition used to create many Christian theological ideas of evil. The symbols that undergird this myth structure are even more important as they show how the mind engages evil to give words to the symbols so that "The Symbol Gives Rise to Thought."[27] Ricoeur's idea

---

24. O'Laughlin, "Closing the Gap," 345.

25. Ricoeur, *Symbolism of Evil*, 174.

26. Ibid., 279.

27. Ibid., 347–48.

of the second naïveté may be useful in engaging Evagrius for this reason.[28] This idea links back to the original symbols of evil, which allows the reader to see the eight thoughts rooted in ancient symbolism. Ricoeur allows us to see that Evagrius had foundations in the Greek philosophical tradition of evil in the same way most Christian theologians have been rooted. By looking at Ricoeur, the work of Evagrius can be seen in a Christian philosophical context, while also getting underneath that context.

Evil and Cognitive Science

In chapter 4 I presented some of the material from Ricoeur and Pierre Changeux in the book *What Makes Us Think?* Because this describes some of Ricoeur's thoughts on evil, I will skip them here, but a general discussion of evil as it relates to the cognitive sciences is useful. Evil has been shown to be a necessary mythical construction of our brains in the work of d'Aquili and Newberg.[29] It can also be the result of a malfunction of our brains, as Ashbrook and Albright have shown.[30] There are many ways that evil can be seen within cognitive science, from a natural malfunction to a normal part of evolutionary life.

In this study, there are two main things that need to be drawn out: one, the brain develops with the need for a myth about evil, and two, evil can be the result of a biological misfire. The ramifications of the latter will be discussed in the constructive section of the study that follows. The former allows us to argue that humans need myths about evil for survival, and that these myths are not limited to a particular theological structure. Newberg and d'Aquili's work lends itself to different theological frameworks and is seen in their use of both Buddhist and Christian meditators. From a Christian perspective, if myth-making is a necessary part of human evolution, then the corresponding part of our brains lends itself to a Christian view of evil that necessitates atonement through the goodness of salvation in Jesus Christ. This is seen in Ricoeur's use of pairs such as "sin-redemption."[31] If there is necessity to create a myth of evil, there is necessity to construct a system of salvation. To clarify, it shows an innate need to categorize things into good and evil groups, a worldview

28. Ibid., 351–52.
29. d'Aquili, Newberg, and Rause, *Why God Won't Go Away*, 62–64.
30. Ashbrook and Albright, *Humanizing Brain*, 157.
31. Ricoeur, *Symbolism of Evil*, 71.

that meshes with Christian theology. I want to be clear that it does not necessitate this viewpoint, but it does mesh with this theological structure.[32] In this study, the most important point to glean is that the mind has a proclivity toward the creation of myth to explain what is good and what is evil. Cognitive science supports the theological position that there is indeed a necessity for a construct of evil.[33]

In regard to the psychotherapy discussion in chapter 4, there is not much of import for this particular discussion of evil, other than to support the idea that it must be battled, or in this case treated. The natural "evil" of brain malfunction can be countered by psychotherapy, and as Kenneth Pargament has shown, this is more beneficial when combined with a spiritual component. Psychotherapy is the next step in encountering evil in the cognitive sciences in that it attempts to treat evil and not just identify it. However, another important distinction to make is that the malfunctioning brain takes the form of anxiety leading to evil behavior.[34] Anxiety is an important part of evil in the mind, specifically moral evil, as psychotherapy is dedicated to combating this evil. Since moral evil is specifically what is important to this study of Evagrius, treating anxiety caused by brain malfunction is at the fore.

In addition, the binary operator of d'Aquili and Newberg may prove useful in Ricoeur's understanding of purity and impurity in the symbols of evil. The cognitive need for humans to understand things in terms of good and evil lends itself to the initial symbol of defilement, where it is not real, but "a symbolic stain."[35] The binary operator groups things into dyads such as good and evil, and is important for the mind to generate myth.[36] The need for the mind to organize input into dyads can connect directly to the foundational symbols of evil in Ricoeur. Thus Newberg

32. This is the difficulty when people speak of the "God spot" because it takes a reductionistic approach to religion. If God can be narrowed into a place in the brain, it either proves that belief in God is a naturalistic phenomenon or that people were "created" for the worship of God. Suffice it to say, the work of d'Aquili and Newberg on the creation of evil myths does not directly look for the "God spot," but their research may be used as such.

33. It is up for debate whether it can answer the question of the existence of true evil, with evil then being an actual entity that is not just a construct of our brains. There is evidence that the construct exists, but beyond this there is room for debate.

34. Ashbrook and Albright, *Humanizing Brain*, 158–62.

35. Ricoeur, *Symbolism of Evil*, 35–37, quotation on 36.

36. d'Aquili and Newberg, *Mystical Mind*, 55.

and d'Aquili's work would seem to support the symbolic approach that Ricoeur takes. This is seen in their proposal that the binary operator constructs dyads for the mind, thus making the world more understandable in the same way that Ricoeur's description of the symbol of defilement does so. The symbol does not have to be literal, but only symbolic, helping the person interpret her world.

The breadth of literature and conjecture regarding evil and the cognitive sciences provides for limitless discussion, but for purposes of this study, there are two major points that have surfaced. Moral evil as it relates to cognitive science stems in part from binary myth formation, as well as brain malfunction.[37] In both cases these descriptions must often be placed on one person by another, as the malfunction or value judgment about a particular behavior must typically be externally viewed by another or in retrospect by the "offender." This, however, is not the case where someone willingly violates her own conscience, causing her to judge her own actions in the negative. Cognitive science supports a structure that allows one to define morality in this way.

Evagrius' Thoughts and Cognitive Science

The last comparative summary that must be made is between the eight thoughts and cognitive science. Since this is the major connection that this study is trying to make, it is most important to delineate before moving on to a constructive synthesis. From the material presented thus far, it is clear that Evagrius has many touchpoints with psychology and the brain. In order to construct a beneficial theology from this study, a bit more interaction with the previous material will be helpful. A good place to start is the large passage from *Chapters on Prayer* quoted in chapter 2. It reads:

> 72. When the mind finally achieves the practice of pure prayer free from the passions, then the demons no longer attack it on the left, but on the right. They suggest to it a notion of God along with some form associated with the senses so that it thinks that it has perfectly attained the goal of prayer. A man experienced in the gnostic life said that this happens under the influence of the

---

37. d'Aquili, Newberg, and Rause, *Why God Won't Go Away*, 63–64. This section discusses the binary operator.

passion of vainglory and that of the demon who touches a place in the brain and causes palpitations in the blood vessels.

73. I think that the demon, by touching the spot just mentioned, alters the light around the mind as he wishes, and in this way the passion of vainglory is moved towards a thought that forms the mind heedlessly towards localizing the divine and essential knowledge. Since the mind is not troubled by the impure passions of the flesh but apparently has a pure disposition, it thinks that there is no longer any contrary activity within it, and so it supposes to be divine the manifestation that arises within it under the influence of the demon, who employs great cunning in altering through the brain the light associated with it and giving the mind a form, as we said previously.[38]

In this passage, there are clear points of contact for modern cognitive science. First, the mention of "the demon who touches a place in the brain and causes palpitations in the blood vessels" is a physical manifestation of an external demonic influence.[39] By stating this, Evagrius is giving nod to the physical, specifically the brain, as he has in other cases by speaking of the burning of the flesh in lust or the restlessness of acedia. The external (demon) has internal and physical influence. This relates to cognitive science and the anxiety that causes malfunction for the brain. The physical/chemical reaction results in poor decision making. Evagrius attributes this to the demonic. The interesting thing in this instance is that the attack on the brain occurs when the monk achieves the state of pure prayer. So even in this advanced state of spirituality, there is still a different kind of evil at work. Even a "healthy" mind can fall prey to vainglory. The good of the person turns to evil through an overconfidence of the defeat of evil.

Second, this passage shows that light is important for Evagrius. Related to this is "the sapphire blue 'light of the mind'" that later surfaces in the Hesychast controversy about a millennia later.[40] Does this relate in some manner to d'Aquili and Newberg's idea of AUB? This link to cognitive science is of great interest, but is far from being empirically shown. The initial work of d'Aquili and Newberg does show some promise on this point, however. In addition, Hesychastic prayer is also referenced in the previous section on Orthodox psychotherapy, and Chrysostomos notes

38. *Chapters on Prayer* 72–73 (Evagrius, *Evagrius of Pontus*, 200–201).

39. Ibid., 200.

40. Stewart, "Practices of Monastic Prayer," 9.

his skepticism at substituting this as a method of therapy.[41] Perhaps it is unfair to relate the two, but it does raise questions. Is there an empirical link between pure prayer and psychotherapeutic treatment? Perhaps not on that ultimate level, but I believe the case can clearly be made on the lower levels of Evagrius' path to the Trinity. Kenneth Pargament's work shows the benefits of the spiritual and the early stages of the Evagrian system deal more with the physical and the disciplined, lending themselves to this type of treatment.

Third, as I initially mentioned, this passage raises the question of spiritual versus physical attacks. What makes this particular reading unique is the mention of the brain. In brain science the malfunction of the brain leading to poor decision-making, as per Ashbrook and Albright, can also be considered in light of the work of Changeux and Ricoeur. Changeux states that "[e]vil is that which opposes survival and society." When the individual takes precedent over the community, this can be seen as evil within an evolutionary perspective.[42] He goes on to say that fear can be used as a survival tool, but also can lead "to abandonment of the social group" causing evil under the previous definition.[43] In this same way, Evagrius' above quote references a place where vainglory, or the uplifting of the individual above other human beings, can come forth even in the place of pure prayer. Likewise, fear and anxiety in biological terms lead to evil just as the other thoughts can cause one to fall to a temptation.

Another interesting connection between cognitive science and the thoughts is that of dreams. Ashbrook and Albright raise the point that lack of REM sleep can cause "disturbed behavior" like disorientation and anxiety.[44] This may have some discussion value for Evagrius' work, for example, where he speaks about dreams in On Thoughts, chapters 27–29. Here he speaks about different types of dreams and how the demons affect a person through dreams.[45] These are not directly linked, but do raise the question of how sleep and dreams are related to anxiety and the thoughts.

41. Chrysostomos, *Guide to Orthodox Psychotherapy*, 99–100. He references Metropolitan Hierotheos' treatment of Hesychasm in contrast to secular psychotherapy.

42. Changeux, and Ricoeur, *What Makes Us Think?*, 280–83, quotation on 281.

43. Ibid., 281–83, quotation on 283.

44. Ashbrook and Albright, *Humanizing Brain*, 96.

45. See Evagrius, *Evagrius of Pontus*, 172–74, specifically 173.

Moving forward, the thoughts are related to each other as has been already shown in the second chapter, and Evagrius has shown them to be systematically vulnerable. Battling the thoughts is an organized endeavor, similar to psychotherapy. Looking at these eight thoughts in dialogue with the cognitive science presented in this study tells us (at least) a few things. First, anxiety affects the brain in biological ways and these can be treated psychotherapeutically. As regards adding a spiritual therapy component, it seems to only benefit treatment. This is shown in the work of Kenneth Pargament and others.

Second, the systematization of Evagrius' attack tends toward the brain's need for order, and the personification of demons is connected to the binary operator of d'Aquili and Newberg. If human survival is based on seeing things as good or bad, then being able to distinguish evil from good in our thoughts is of the utmost importance. Evagrius' system, rooted in Greek philosophy, brings one closer to this goal. It allows one to distinguish evil thoughts and rid oneself of them, while moving closer to communion with God in prayer. The language is disparate between Evagrius and modern science, yet the steps of prayer and discipline can be useful to ease the worries of the mind. Many Christian believers would assent to this, even if they cannot show it to be true empirically. This creates a sort of practical reality to the spiritual approach to psychotherapy. As Pargament shows, empirical research supports the fact that this approach is equally, if not more, beneficial. The reasons for this however, are a bit more murky.

Third, Newberg and d'Aquili's research in the attempt to find "Absolute Unitary Being" adds some empirical backing to Evagrius' system of prayer. Although their research is an attempt to show more than just his "place of pure prayer," it does tend to enhance the notion that Evagrius' system has some empirical support. The reasons for reaching this place of meditation may not be the same reasons that Evagrius writes about, but empirically, the brain is doing something when higher states of meditation are reached.

These three places are the major contact points for Evagrius and cognitive science: binary operation, AUB, and spiritually integrated psychotherapy. This is in addition to the general connections between the mind under duress that is a part of both cognitive science and the writings of the monk. The broader connections between evil and cognitive science have already been drawn out and have limitless possibilities for conversation.

The details have already been presented in chapters 2–4 and these major touchpoints can be gleaned from this study. This allows for a constructive conversation about evil drawing from these sources. What does all of this mean, and how does the research presented help us to create descriptions about moral evil in the human and the broader world?

Constructing a Dialogical Approach to the Discussion of Evil

Now that all of this research has been set out on the table, where does this leave us? There are two major syntheses that should follow from the study already presented in this text. First, one should see why Evagrius is relevant to the theology and science dialogue, specifically as it relates to a theological discussion of evil and prayer. Second, there is the overarching dialogical approach to three different topics: Evagrius' eight thoughts, evil, and cognitive science, which must be sifted to create new and helpful statements about the nature of moral evil as it relates to theology.

Evagrius, Evil, and Science and Theology Dialogue

Before moving into the broader theological constructs, it is beneficial to speak about the synthesis of the topics in this study and their use in science and theology dialogue. We have already seen the touchpoints of this book as it relates to the eight thoughts and cognitive science, focusing especially on the work of d'Aquili and Newberg. The previous section has given a summary of this work. Although not totally satisfying, their work along with that of Kenneth Pargament show that gains are being made in the scientific realm to support that there is empirical data to justify the benefit and results of the practices of which Evagrius speaks: both to show higher mystical states and the benefit of spirituality in treating mental disease. Combining this with a discussion of Orthodox psychotherapy, one sees that patristics and psychotherapy do have many connections, although many times their purposes may be different. To do a full study of Evagrius' work on the thoughts as it relates to psychotherapy would take an exegetical piece of work that would be much more detail oriented than I can offer here. However, there are at least four concepts that can be drawn from this study that relate to theological discourse in science and theology.

First, patristics can be used as a research partner in theology and science. By patristics I am referring predominately to pre-medieval writers dating up through the time of John of Damascus. Occasionally patristics is allowed into the arena of science and theology, but quite often it is ignored, perhaps because it is not a post-Enlightenment area of study. One example of this engagement is the text by Alexei Nesteruk, *Light from the East*, which shows major usage of patristic sources, but also comes from an Eastern perspective, as might be expected.[46] Western Christians would also be wise to engage the work of the church fathers even if it is not a necessary part of systematic theology for many as it is in the East. The fathers offer insight into both the spiritual life of the Christian and the formation of doctrines that are foundational to subsequent theology. Thus they offer both practical and theoretical theological concepts. This study of Evagrius' eight thoughts shows specific engagement with a patristic writer's work as it has relation to the modern sciences. There are limitless topics available in the patristic world that relate to science and nature, from the *Hexameron* of Basil to the same work of Ambrose to the discussions of time and eternity in Augustine's *Confessions*. The patristic writers were often active with the "science" of their time, usually in the form of Greek philosophy, and make excellent dialogue partners. In Evagrius' work, this is evident in the many quotations and descriptions already mentioned.

Second, the metaphors used in Evagrius' writings are relevant to the human pursuit of theological truth. An example of this can be found in the thoughts themselves. Another name for the thoughts is the demons. Evagrius writes about external demons that affect the monk in his pursuit of God. Whether or not one literally believes in demonic beings that roam the earth looking to tempt people to do evil, the metaphor of the demonic is helpful because it gives personification to evil and thus makes it easier to battle. When an adversary is identified, only then can combat truly begin. This personification allows one to feel as if they are battling a physical enemy, which at times may be easier than fighting an unknown anxiety. The unknown often causes more fear than the known, and in many cases this supernatural identification may be helpful. This follows from the discussion on myth formation and evil in the work of d'Aquili and Newberg. They identify a binary operator that allows one to

46. Nesteruk has also published a more recent volume, *The Universe as Communion*, in which he discusses theology and science in the context of Christian tradition and patristic thought. Nesteruk is one of the few authors discussing patristics in the context of theology and science.

place things into either/or categories, thus maximizing a person's chance at survival.[47] In following Evagrius' work, the road to God is more easily attained through the battle with the demons, as well as with oneself.[48] This is true of all supernatural language, but one must also be careful when applying this language to psychotherapy, as Chrysostomos has cautioned. In the battle against moral evil, giving language to this struggle is useful and can be learned from the patristic fathers, specifically Evagrius.

Third, Ricoeur's idea of a "second naïveté" is useful in rereading Evagrius' work. Just as with the previous point made, scholars often dismiss the pre-modern language as out of touch or inaccurate, without a full understanding of what is being said. The idea of a second naïveté aims to recapture this understanding and see it again with fresh eyes. As Ricoeur states, "I believe that being can still speak to me—no longer, of course, under the precritical form of immediate belief, but as the second immediacy aimed at by hermeneutics."[49] He goes on to make a distinction between "dymythologizing" and "demythicizing," with the former allowing one to get at the objective truth.[50] Often in the scientific world, the pre-modern has been dismissed as an old way of understanding something, but through hermeneutic recovery one may see truth that connects with current science and theology. It is in this connection that there is hope for patristic dialogue with religion and science, as is made clear in the example

47. d'Aquili, Newberg, and Rause, *Why God Won't Go Away*, 63–64. Black-and-white categories can also be problematic, as many things in regard to evil are, at times, "gray." Dividing into binary categories is helpful for simplification of many dangers and evils, but must be done in an educated manner, acknowledging the danger of this approach. One must not place things into categories hastily. On 63 the authors are emphasizing the dyadic pairs used in myth making, allowing sensory inputs to the brain to be better managed and helping the person to make sense of his or her environment. In the same way, supernatural language can help Christian believers make sense of their faith and challenges by placing them in language structures that create a combat motif.

48. Using both "thoughts" and "demons" to describe Evagrius' eight thoughts has merit in that they each work in some contexts better than others. To make the point of the use of metaphor and personification, I have chosen to use demons here. In discussion of cognitive science and the mind, "thoughts" may work better.

49. Ricoeur, *Symbolism of Evil*, 351–52, quotation on 352. This approach allows for the reader of Evagrian texts to get behind the lack of modern, scientific language to try to understand what is Evagrius' intended meaning. It also allows for new meanings to be imposed upon the text that may be helpful, though not in the author's original intent. Choosing a method to interpret texts as a whole, however, is a discussion for a separate hermeneutical study.

50. Ibid., 352–53.

of Evagrius and psychotherapy. Hermeneutic recovery allows a reader to capture meaning that otherwise would be lost due to the obstacle of critical interpretation. We have lost the "immediate belief" that Ricoeur mentions, but can still learn from and accept the pre-modern in many cases.

Fourth, Ricoeur's idea of a "semantic dualism" is helpful in understanding the usefulness of Evagrius' texts. I would prefer to use the term *practical dualism* as I think practicality is also important to using Evagrius' work in a modern scientific world. Ricoeur seems to present semantic dualism as a "dualism of discourses" instead of a "dualism of substances," but that the former often moves toward the latter.[51] He goes on to show how the former becomes the latter. He states,

> Thus, I can say that my hands, my feet, and so forth are my organs in the sense that I walk with my feet, I grasp with my hands—but this comes under the head of personal experience, and I do not have to commit myself to an ontology of the soul in order to speak in this way. By contrast, when I am told that I have a brain, no actual experience corresponds to this; I learn about it in books—[52]

He also discusses the difference in this type of knowledge, giving the example of one using one's hands versus thinking with one's brain, as he did prior to this statement. Here Ricoeur shows that it is impossible to speak of the thoughts and brain and neurology without a language that has been taught to us, imposed upon us, versus the experience of standing on our legs or moving our arms.[53] Thus it is necessary to speak in at least a semantic dualism, because we are forced to deal with this knowledge-based reality, i.e., being told that we think with our brain, that does not hold in our experience. Changeux follows this up by clarifying that Ricoeur is speaking of two different languages: one for anatomy, which includes the brain and neurology, and one for behavior, thought, emotion, etc.[54] Ultimately Ricoeur defends a semantic dualism that separates the "personal experience" of the individual and "all the ways of objectifying integral human experience."[55]

---

51. Changeux and Ricoeur, *What Makes Us Think?*, 14.

52. Ibid., 15–16.

53. Ibid., 16.

54. Ibid., 16–17.

55. Ibid., 27. This line of thought continues with interaction from Changeux until p. 30.

In my formation of a practical dualism, I believe that in order to discuss the wholeness of a person it is necessary to talk about the material and immaterial parts of a person. This does not necessarily mean that a person has a separate soul or is composed of two distinct parts as Evagrius may have said. It does mean that it is helpful to speak in this way, however, to do justice to the spiritual aspects of persons and not reduce them to a biological machine where their very consciousness is just a grouping of chemical reactions. The practical aspect follows Ricoeur's discussion of personal experience, where the individual's immaterial thoughts and behaviors can be discussed differently than their body. This could just be a semantic distinction, which for the most part seems to be what Ricoeur is after, but in practicality it is a reality. When engaging texts like Evagrius' writings on prayer and the thoughts, this distinction is helpful. It is, however, interesting that Evagrius also uses language that supports the connection and wholeness of body and mind, as is evident in the block quote earlier in this chapter. Evagrius is embodying the same dilemma that we engage in modern science: he is using the "science" of his day to describe the experiences he has in the spiritual realm. His cosmology, following from the ancient Greeks, is clearly the language used to describe his own spiritual journey. This parallels the modern religion and science dialogue and the "problem" of dualism. The language we draw upon from our scientific knowledge frames the discussion. In this same way, reading Evagrius offers a caution to modern religion and science enthusiasts: do not get caught up in the current language to the extent it limits understanding, but at the same time use this same language to better understand humanity's spiritual relationships.

There are many more ways to connect Evagrius' work with that of science and theology, but these four offer a good platform to begin. The depth of his work should not be minimized due to the fact that "science" has changed so much since the fourth century. There are overarching concepts that come through to the present, above and beyond the initial connections we have already made. Prayer and moral struggle are examples of these conceptual parts of the spiritual life that have always been a part of historical Christianity.

Broader Statements about Moral Evil

In addition to the prior statements drawn from the dialogue between Evagrius and cognitive science regarding the science-theology dialogue, it is beneficial to revisit some of the descriptors of evil from chapter 3 and show how this study has furthered those definitions of evil. Before addressing this, however, there is another overarching theme that must be addressed, which is that of the limitations of science for this study in describing evil in the mind/brain.

The question, has been raised previously, specifically in the work of Ashbrook and Albright, of why some people choose to do good in the face of anxiety or stress. They raise the point that some "have endured the most wretched catastrophes without falling apart," affirming that "[i]ntentionality is still the core of humanity," using Jesus as the best example. In other words, human actions are not predetermined. Free will plays a role. Humans can be intentional about the decisions they make in the face of stress.[56] They underscore the balance between reason and emotion for the health of the brain.[57] As stated earlier, when the defense system malfunctions under extreme stress it can cause people to act in evil ways.[58] How can humans act for good when their reactions are to do evil, perceiving it to be good? This intentionality that they speak of is exactly the sort of behavior that Evagrius' disciplines instill in the Christian. With the help of the Holy Spirit, this allows a person to overcome their "nature" and do what is good.

The main reason I raise this point is to say that science may tell us how a brain reacts to anxiety or the evolutionary benefits of distinguishing good and evil, as stated in d'Aquili and Newberg, but it does not answer the question why people sometimes choose to do good when evil is the natural response. Newberg, d'Aquili, and Rause state, "The best that science can give us is a metaphorical picture of what's real, and while that picture may make sense, it isn't necessarily true."[59] They hold that science and religion are both "powerful but incomplete pathways to the same ultimate reality."[60] Although I disagree with their assumption that these

56. Ashbrook and Albright, *Humanizing Brain*, 162, including both quotations.
57. Ibid., 158.
58. Ibid., 158–61.
59. d'Aquili, Newberg, and Rause, *Why God Won't Go Away*, 170.
60. Ibid., 168–69, quotation on 169.

paths lead to the same ultimate reality, it is clear that science does not give a full picture of truth. It is limited by its own parameters of inquiry. In the end, they state, "The realness of Absolute Unitary Being is not conclusive proof that a higher God exists, but it makes a strong case that there is more to human existence than sheer material existence."[61] Although I do not think that AUB proves the existence of God or of mystical states, it does show that these states could be part of a natural mind/brain process. Again, science does not tell the whole story, even in the case of validating religious experience. It does, however, add to our breadth of knowledge.

Part of the function of this text has been to connect the writings of Evagrius and cognitive science empirically, if only by parallel. Thus, implicitly, I have argued that scientific truth is a valid means of obtaining truth. The other side to this is that I am arguing for the scientific empirical data regarding mysticism and spirituality in order to draw Evagrius' writings into deeper dialogue with the scientific community. I have chosen to accept research that applies the scientific method to religious thought in the hope that it will draw the two closer together. The validity of Evagrius' work goes far beyond the assumptions of science, but part of the hope in this research is to validate the practical aspects of Evagrius' spiritual quest and worldview through empirical methods. However, this is only part of the task, which is why the limitations of the scientific approach must be noted here.

To move back to Ashbrook and Albright's statements about why people act for the good of everyone even in the face of extreme stress, this is where science does not always offer complete answers.[62] Some may argue this is truly for the good of evolutionary survival, but is it? Theology helps us to address some of these issues. I have chosen to avoid discussion on the nature of humanity in this study as it is a limitless topic of great depth and would take away from the work on Evagrius, but questions about human nature will always be interpreted in light of scientific evidence. The eight thoughts may not use scientific language, but in a practical sense, they can be shown to have spiritual and physical value for the health of a person. This study is just one more link to this deeper conversation between science and theology.

---

61. Ibid., 172.
62. Ashbrook and Albright, *Humanizing Brain*, 162.

This study has focused on building bridges between Christian spirituality and empirical science, while showing the use and depth of patristic work in dialogue with science and theology. The broader questions cannot be answered in one fell swoop. This study has attempted to build bridges to give a fuller account of what evil is for one ascetic monk, a Christian philosopher, and select scholars in the cognitive sciences, and to blend their work and show where there are dialogical connections. The cognitive sciences do not prove mystical experience, nor do they prove the existence of evil. They do, however, help us to describe these things, adding more dimensions to our understanding of them.

Conclusion

As stated, this study has constructed connections between a patristic theologian and select cognitive sciences. The work of d'Aquili and Newberg as well as that of Kenneth Pargament is still in the early stages. There is clear evidence for the possibility of empirically shown higher states of meditation as well as the use of spiritual practices in psychotherapy. The symbols of evil that Ricoeur has given us lay foundations that are vital to dialogical theology in regard to evil. The eight thoughts of Evagrius are important for many spiritual practices as we see in Orthodox psychotherapy.

This study has shown the fruit that is to be borne by placing patristics in dialogue with post-Enlightenment science within the religion-science dialogue. The work of Evagrius on the thoughts opens up conversational possibilities with neuroscience and psychology. As stated above, there are three major touchpoints in regard to the eight thoughts: binary operation, AUB, and spiritually integrated psychotherapy. These connections show the fruit of this study and help to build toward a better overall discussion of evil and prayer within the religion and science community, yet this is only a beginning.

To reiterate what I mentioned in the beginning of this chapter, this study has predominately been addressed to Christians who are confessional but may still have doubts about various supernatural aspects of Christianity. Believers that see science as the final arbiter of truth often have difficulties with these areas. It is with wariness that they approach discussions of demons and other "supernatural" language because of the underlying Enlightenment assumptions that undergird their outlook. As I stated at the beginning of this chapter, the main focus of this study has been on bringing Evagrius' writings on evil and prayer into conversation with current cognitive science in an attempt to better understand his writings and see that they have merit for the Christian who struggles with anxiety and moral evil. Again, it is my wish that this book has helped to present empirical support and hope to those who wish to understand the spiritual life better. Anxiety and moral evil have always been difficulties of the Christian life, and prayer and Scripture are two of the most important tools in combating these obstacles to spiritual health. This study also offers some scientific evidence for mysticism, and although this may be helpful to some, and it is my hope that it is, I leave the interpretation of the validity of mystic experiences up to the reader. I wish to conclude by emphasizing the use of prayer to combat anxiety, and making use of supernatural language as an acceptable context for combating this evil.

It is also my hope that, in addition to the skeptical Christian, there are items of interest to the non-believer, meaning one who does not hold to any confession of the Trinity or the person of Jesus Christ. There is evidence for a scientific existence of mystical experiences, and the current data can be interpreted in various ways. Despite this, there is enough evidence to show that many who speak of demons and connection with God have some empirical support. In undertaking a study of this sort, the results will never be as conclusive as one might like. To overlay the empirical upon a theological structure will either end in limiting the theological system or not meeting the scientific burden of proof. In this study, I have attempted to show that there is empirical evidence that Evagrius' work has merit in current Christian theology, and tried to open a pathway of dialogue for his writings with modern cognitive science. This does not mean that one must accept his beliefs wholesale, and I certainly do not, but hopefully it makes his writings relevant for our construction of Christian theology.

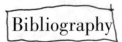
Bibliography

Albright, Carol Rausch. "Neurotheology." In *Science, Religion, and Society: An Encyclopedia of History, Culture, and Controversy*, vol. 2, edited by Arri Eisen and Gary Laderman, 536–42. Armonk, NY: M. E. Sharpe, 2007.

———. "Religion as a Dynamic Process: Cognition, Complexification, and Spiritual Growth." Paper presented to the Advanced Seminar in Religion and Science at the Lutheran School of Theology at Chicago, April 28, 2004.

Albright, Carol Rausch, and James B. Ashbrook. *Where God Lives in the Human Brain*. Naperville, IL: Sourcebooks, 2001.

Andresen, Jensine. "Conclusion: Religion in the Flesh: Forging New Methodologies for the Study of Religion." In *Religion in Mind: Cognitive Perspectives on Religious Belief, Ritual, and Experience*, edited by Jensine Andresen, 257–87. Cambridge: Cambridge University Press, 2001.

———. "Introduction: Towards a Cognitive Science of Religion." In *Religion in Mind: Cognitive Perspectives on Religious Belief, Ritual, and Experience*, edited by Jensine Andresen, 1–44. Cambridge: Cambridge University Press, 2001.

Ante-Nicene Fathers. Vol. 1, *The Apostolic Fathers, Justin Martyr, Irenaeus*. Edited by Alexander Roberts and James Donaldson, revised by A. Cleveland Coxe. 1885. Reprint, Peabody, MA: Hendrickson, 1999.

Ashbrook, James B., and Carol Rausch Albright. *The Humanizing Brain: Where Religion and Neuroscience Meet*. Cleveland, OH: Pilgrim, 1997.

Augustine. "The Grace of Christ and Original Sin." In *Answer to the Pelagians*, edited and translated with an introduction by Roland J. Teske, 384–463. The Works of Saint Augustine: A Translation for the 21st Century, pt. 1, vol. 23. Hyde Park, NY: New City, 1997.

———. *On Free Choice of the Will*. Translated by Thomas Williams. Indianapolis: Hackett, 1993.

———. "Grace and Free Choice." In *Answer to the Pelagians IV*, edited by translated by Roland J. Teske, 70–106. The Works of Saint Augustine: A Translation for the 21st Century, pt. 1, vol. 26. Hyde Park, NY: New City, 1999.

Barciauskas, Rosemary Curran. "The Primordial and Ethical Interpretations of Evil in Paul Ricoeur and Alfred North Whitehead." *Modern Theology* 2.1 (1985) 64–77.

i.e. created, material

Barrett, Justin. "Exploring the Natural Foundations of Religion." *Trends in Cognitive Science* 4.1 (2000) 29–34.

Beauregard, Mario, and Denyse O'Leary. *The Spiritual Brain: A Neuroscientist's Case for the Existence of the Soul*. New York: HarperOne, 2007.

Bennett, Patrick R., and Marta Elliott, "God Give Me Strength: Exploring the Impact of Prayer as Self-Disclosure to God on Emotion and Physical Health." Unpublished paper, 2007.

Blocher, Henri. *Evil and the Cross*. Translated buyDavid G. Preston. Downers Grove, IL: InterVarsity, 1994.

Boyer, Pascal. "Religious Thought and Behaviour as By-Products of Brain Function." *TRENDS in Cognitive Sciences* 7.3 (2003) 119–24.

Brakke, David. "Monks, Priests, and Magicians: Demons and Monastic Self-Differentiation in Late Ancient Egypt." Paper presented at the "Living for Eternity" conference, University of Minnesota, March 7, 2003.

Brenton, Charles Lee. *The Septuagint Version of the Old Testament and Apocrypha. With an English Translation and with Various Readings and Critical Notes*. 1851. Reprint, Grand Rapids: Zondervan, 1978.

Brown, Warren S. "Cognitive Contributions to Soul." In *Whatever Happened to the Soul? Scientific and Theological Portraits of Human Nature*, edited by Warren S. Brown, Nancey Murphy, and H. Newton Malony, 99–125. Theology and the Sciences. Minneapolis: Fortress, 1998.

Burrus, Virginia. "Praying Is Joying: Musings on Love in Evagrius Ponticus." In *Toward a Theology of Eros: Transfiguring Passion at the Limits of Discipline*, edited by Virginia Burrus and Catherine Keller, 194–204. Transdisciplinary Theological Colloquia. New York: Fordham University Press, 2006.

Casiday, Augustine. "Deification in Origen, Evagrius, and Cassian." In *Origeniana Octava: Origen and the Alexandrian Tradition; Papers of the 8th International Origen Congress, Pisa, 27–31 August 2001*, edited by L. Perrone, 2:995–1001. Bibliotheca Ephemeridum theologicarum Lovaniensium 164. Leuven: Leuven University Press, 2003.

———, editor. *Evagrius Ponticus*. Early Church Fathers. New York: Routledge, 2006.

———. "Gabriel Bunge and the Study of Evagrius Ponticus." *St. Vladimir's Theological Quarterly* 48.2–3 (2004) 249–97.

Center for the Study of Health, Religion, and Spirituality, Indiana State University. http://www1.indstate.edu/psychology/cshrs.htm.

Changeux, Jean-Pierre, and Paul Ricoeur. *What Makes Us Think? A Neuroscientist and a Philosopher Argue about Ethics, Human Nature, and the Brain*. Translated by M. B. DeBevoise. Princeton, NJ: Princeton University Press, 2000.

Chrysostomos, Archbishop of Etna. *A Guide to Orthodox Psychotherapy: The Science, Theology, and Spiritual Practice behind It and Its Clinical Applications*. Lanham, MD: University Press of America, 2007.

Clark, Elizabeth A. *The Origenist Controversy: The Cultural Construction of an Early Christian Debate*. Princeton, NJ: Princeton University Press, 1992.

Cooper, Robert M. "Saint Augustine's Doctrine of Evil." *Scottish Journal of Theology* 16.3 (1963) 256–76.

Cooper, Terry D. *Dimensions of Evil: Contemporary Perspectives*. Minneapolis: Fortress, 2007.

d'Aquili, Eugene G., and Andrew B. Newberg. *The Mystical Mind: Probing the Biology of Religious Experience*. Theology and the Sciences. Minneapolis: Fortress, 1999.

d'Aquili, Eugene G., Andrew B. Newberg, and Vince Rause. *Why God Won't Go Away: Brain Science and the Biology of Belief*. New York: Ballantine, 2001.

Davis, Stephen T. "Free Will and Evil." In *Encountering Evil: Live Options in Theodicy*, edited by Stephen T. Davis, 73–89, 101–7. New ed. Louisville: Westminster John Knox, 2001.

Duffy, Stephen J. "Genes, Original Sin and the Human Proclivity to Evil." *Horizons* 32.2 (2005) 210–34.

Dysinger, Luke. *Psalmody and Prayer in the Writings of Evagrius Ponticus*. Oxford Theological Monographs. Oxford: Oxford University Press, 2005.

Evagrius Ponticus. *Evagrius of Pontus: The Greek Ascetic Corpus*. Translation, commentary, and introduction by Robert E. Sinkewicz. Oxford Early Christian Studies. Oxford: Oxford University Press, 2003.

———. *Evagrius Ponticus: Ad Monachos*. Translation and commentary by Jeremy Driscoll. Ancient Christian Writers 59. Mahwah, NJ: Newman, 2003.

———. *The Praktikos. Chapters on Prayer*. Cistercian Studies 4. Translation, notes, and introduction by John Eudes Bamberger. Kalamazoo, MI: Cistercian, 1981.

Evans, G. R. *Augustine on Evil*. Cambridge: Cambridge University Press, 1982.

Gaiser, Frederick J. "Paul Ricoeur's Myth of Evil in Biblical Perspective." *Word & World* 19.4 (1999) 389–400.

Geddes, Jennifer L., editor. *Evil after Postmodernism: Histories, Narratives and Ethics*. New York: Routledge, 2001.

Gerhart, Mary. "Paul Ricoeur's Notion of 'Diagnostics': Its Function in Literary Interpretation." *Journal of Religion* 56.2 (1976) 137–56.

Goldingay, John. "Covenant, OT and NT." In *The New Interpreter's Dictionary of the Bible*, edited by Katharine Doob Sakenfeld, 1:767–78. Nashville: Abingdon, 2006.

Graves, Mark. *Mind, Brain and the Elusive Soul: Human Systems of Cognitive Science and Religion*. Ashgate Science and Religion Series. Aldershot, England: Ashgate, 2008.

Grenz, Stanley J., and Roger E. Olson. *20th Century Theology: God & the World in a Transitional Age*. Downers Grove, IL: InterVarsity, 1992.

Hadot, Pierre. *Philosophy as a Way of Life: Spiritual Exercises from Socrates to Foucault*. Edited with an introduction by Arnold Davidson, translated by Michael Chase. Oxford: Blackwell, 1995.

———. *Plotinus, or, The Simplicity of Vision*. Translated by Michael Chase. Chicago: University of Chicago Press, 1998.

———. *What Is Ancient Philosophy?* Translated by Michael Chase. Cambridge, MA: Belknap Press of Harvard University Press, 2002.

Harmless, William. *Desert Christians: An Introduction to the Literature of Early Monasticism*. New York: Oxford University Press, 2004.

Hefner, Philip. "The Problem of Evil: Picking Up the Pieces." *Dialog* 25 (Spring 1986) 87–92.

———. "Reflecting on Cognitive Science and Religion." Presentation to the Advanced Seminar in Religion and Science at the Lutheran School of Theology at Chicago, March 31, 2004.

Hick, John. *Evil and the God of Love*. 2nd ed. New York: Palgrave Macmillan, 2007.

Hill, Peter C., and Kenneth I. Pargament. "Advances in the Conceptualization and Measurement of Religion and Spirituality: Implications for Physical and Mental Health Research." *American Psychologist* 58.1 (2003) 64–74.

Hogue, David A. *Remembering the Future, Imagining the Past: Story, Ritual, and the Human Brain.* Cleveland: Pilgrim, 2003.

Hollinger, David A. "James, Clifford, and the Scientific Conscience." In *The Cambridge Companion to William James*, edited by Ruth Anna Putnam, 69–83. New York: Cambridge University Press, 1997.

Idhe, Don. *Hermeneutic Phenomenology: The Philosophy of Paul Ricoeur.* Forward by Paul Ricoeur. Northwestern University Studies in Phenomenology & Existential Philosophy. Evanston: Northwestern University Press, 1971.

James, William. *The Varieties of Religious Experience: A Study in Human Nature.* Centenary ed. New York: Routledge, 2002.

Jeeves, Malcom. "Brain, Mind, and Behavior." In *Whatever Happened to the Soul? Scientific and Theological Portraits of Human Nature*, edited by Warren S. Brown, Nancey Murphy, and H. Newton Malony, 73–98. Theology and the Sciences. Minneapolis: Fortress, 1998.

Kant, Immanuel. "Concerning the Indwelling of the Evil Principle with the Good, or, On the Radical Evil in Human Nature." In *Religion within the Limits of Reason Alone*, translated with an introduction by Theodore M. Greene and Hoyt H. Hudson, 15–49. New York: Harper & Row, 1960.

Kearney, Richard. "On the Hermeneutics of Evil." In *Reading Ricoeur*, edited by David M. Kaplan, 71–88. Albany: SUNY Press, 2008.

LaCocque, André, and Paul Ricoeur. *Thinking Biblically: Exegetical and Hermeneutical Studies.* Translated by David Pellauer. Chicago: University of Chicago Press, 1998.

Livingston, James C. *Modern Christian Thought.* Vol. 1, *The Enlightenment and the Nineteenth Century.* Minneapolis: Fortress, 2006.

Louth, Andrew. *The Origins of the Christian Mystical Tradition from Plato to Denys.* New York: Oxford University Press, 1981.

————. *Wisdom of the Byzantine Church: Evagrios of Pontos and Maximos the Confessor.* Edited by Jill Raitt. Paine Lectures in Religion, 1997. Columbia, MO: Department of Religious Studies, University of Missouri, 1998.

Mathewes, Charles T. *Evil and the Augustinian Tradition.* Cambridge: Cambridge University Press, 2001.

McCauley, Robert N., and Thomas E. Lawson. *Bringing Ritual to Mind: Psychological Foundations of Cultural Forms.* Cambridge: Cambridge University Press, 2002.

McGinn, Bernard. "Asceticism and the Emergence of the Monastic Tradition." In *Asceticism*, edited by Vincent L. Wimbush and Richard Valantasis, 58–74. New York: Oxford University Press, 1995.

Midgley, Mary. "How Myths Work." In *God and Evolution: A Reader*, edited by Mary Kathleen Cunningham, 28–33. New York: Routledge, 2007.

Moreland, J. P. "The Mind-Body Problem." In *Science, Religion, and Society: An Encyclopedia of History, Culture, and Controversy*, vol. 2, edited by Arri Eisen and Gary Laderman, 565–74. Armonk, NY: M. E. Sharpe, 2007.

Neiman, Susan. *Evil in Modern Thought: An Alternative History of Philosophy.* Princeton, NJ: Princeton University Press, 2002.

Nesteruk, Alexei V. *Light from the East: Theology, Science, and the Eastern Orthodox Tradition.* Theology and the Sciences. Minneapolis: Fortress, 2003.

————. *The Universe as Communion: Towards a Neo-patristic Synthesis of Theology and Science.* London: T. & T. Clark, 2008.

xerox

Newhauser, Richard. "Introduction: Cultural Construction and the Vices." In *The Seven Deadly Sins: From Communities to Individuals*, edited by Richard Newhauser, 1–17. Studies in Medieval and Reformation Traditions 123. Leiden: Brill, 2007.

Niebuhr, Reinhold. *The Nature and Destiny of Man: A Christian Interpretation*. 2 vols. Library of Theological Ethics. Louisville: Westminster John Knox, 1996.

Niebuhr, Richard R. "William James on Religious Experience." In *The Cambridge Companion to William James*, edited by Ruth Anna Putnam, 214–36. New York: Cambridge University Press, 1997.

O'Laughlin, Michael. "Closing the Gap between Antony and Evagrius." In *Origeniana Septima: Origenes in den Auseinandersetzungen des 4. Jahrhunderts*. W. A. Bienert and U. Kühneweg, 345–54. Bibliotheca Ephemeridum theologicarum Lovaniensium 137. Leuven: Leuven University Press, 1999.

———. "New Questions Concerning the Origenism of Evagrius." In *Origeniana Quinta: Historica, Text and Method, Biblica, Philosophica, Theologica, Origenism and Later Developments; Papers of the 5th International Origen Congress, Boston College, 14–18 August 1989*, edited by Robert J. Daly, 528–34. Bibliotheca Ephemeridum theologicarum Lovaniensium 105. Leuven: Leuven University Press, 1992.

Pagels, Elaine H. *Adam, Eve, and the Serpent*. New York: Vintage, 1988.

Pargament, Kenneth I. *Spiritually Integrated Psychotherapy: Understanding and Addressing the Sacred*. New York: Guilford, 2007.

Pargament, Kenneth I., Nichole A. Murray-Swank, Gina M. Magyar, and Gene G. Ano. "Spiritual Struggle: A Phenomenon of Interest to Psychology and Religion." In *Judeo-Christian Perspectives on Psychology: Human Nature, Motivation, and Change*, edited by William R. Miller and Harold D. Delaney, 245–68. Washington DC: American Psychological Association. 2005.

Pelikan, Jaroslav. *Christianity and Classical Culture: The Metamorphosis of Natural Theology in the Christian Encounter with Hellenism*. New Haven: Yale University Press, 1993.

Persinger, Michael A. *Neuropsychological Bases of God Beliefs*. New York: Praeger, 1987.

Peters, Ted. *Sin: Radical Evil in Soul and Society*. Grand Rapids: Eerdmans, 1994.

Peterson, Greg, Michael L. Spezio, and James Van Slyke. Presentation to the Science, Technology, and Religion Group (theme: "Neuroscience, Transcendence, and Moral Exemplars") at the American Academy of Religion 2008 Annual Meeting, November 2, 2008.

Peterson, Gregory R. *Minding God: Theology and the Cognitive Sciences*. Theology and the Sciences. Minneapolis: Fortress, 2003.

Ramachandran, V. S., and Sandra Blakeslee. *Phantoms in the Brain: Probing the Mysteries of the Human Mind*. New York: William Morrow, 1998.

Ricoeur, Paul. "Evil, a Challenge to Philosophy and Theology." Translated by David Pellauer. *Journal of the American Academy of Religion* 53.4 (December 1985) 635–48.

———. *Evil: A Challenge to Philosophy and Theology*. Translated by John Bowden. New York: Continuum, 2007.

———. "Original Sin: A Study in Meaning." Translated by Peter McCormick. In *The Conflict of Interpretations: Essays in Hermeneutics*, edited by Don Ihde, 269–86. New ed. Northwestern University Studies in Phenomenology & Existential Philosophy. Evanston, IL: Northwestern University Press, 2007.

———. *The Symbolism of Evil*. Translated by Emerson Buchanan. Boston: Beacon, 1969.

Rogozinski, Jacob. "It Makes Us Wrong: Kant and Radical Evil." Translated by Debra Keates. In *Radical Evil*, edited by Joan Copjec, 30–45. New York: Verso, 1996.

Runehov, Anne L. C. *Sacred or Neural? The Potential of Neuroscience to Explain Religious Experience*. Religion, Theologie und Naturwissenschaft 9. Göttingen: Vandenhoeck & Ruprecht, 2007.

Russell, Robert John. "Entropy and Evil." *Zygon* 19.4 (1984) 449–68.

Sands, Kathleen M. *Escape from Paradise: Evil and Tragedy in Feminist Theology*. Minneapolis: Fortress, 1994.

Schwarz, Hans. *Evil: A Historical and Theological Perspective*. Translated by Mark W. Worthing. 1995. Reprint, Lima, OH: Academic Renewal, 2001.

Solomon, Andrew. *The Noonday Demon: An Atlas of Depression*. New York: Scribner, 2001.

Somos, Róbert. "Origen, Evagrius Ponticus and the Ideal of Impassibility." In *Origeniana Septima: Origenes in den Auseinandersetzungen des 4. Jahrhunderts*. W. A. Bienert and U. Kühneweg, 365–73. Bibliotheca Ephemeridum theologicarum Lovaniensium 137. Leuven: Leuven University Press, 1999.

Stewart, Columba. *Cassian the Monk*. Oxford Studies in Historical Theology. New York: Oxford University Press, 1998.

———. "Evagrius Ponticus on Prayer and Anger." In *Religions of Late Antiquity in Practice*, edited by Richard Valantasis, 65–81. Princeton Readings in Religions. Princeton: Princeton University Press, 2000.

———. "Imageless Prayer and the Theological Vision of Evagrius Ponticus." *Journal of Early Christian Studies* 9.2 (2001) 173–204.

———. "The Practices of Monastic Prayer: Origins, Evolution, and Tensions." Paper delivered at the "Living for Eternity" conference, University of Minnesota, March 7, 2003.

Tillich, Paul. *Systematic Theology*. Vol. 2, *Existence and the Christ*. Chicago: University of Chicago Press, 1957.

Turner, H. J. M. "Evagrius Ponticus, Teacher of Prayer." *Eastern Churches Review* 7.2 (1975) 145–48.

Underwood, Geoffrey, editor. *The Oxford Guide to the Mind*. Oxford: Oxford University Press, 2001.

Vlachos, Hierotheos S., Metropolitan of Nafpaktos. *Orthodox Psychotherapy: The Science of the Fathers*. Translated by Esther Williams. Levadia, Greece: Birth of the Theotokos Monastery, 1994.

Ware, Kallistos. "The Way of the Ascetics: Negative or Affirmative?" In *Asceticism*, edited by Vincent L. Wimbush and Richard Valantasis, 3–15. New York: Oxford University Press, 1995.

Watts, Fraser N., editor. *Perspectives on Prayer*. London: SPCK, 2001.

———. *Theology and Psychology*. Ashgate Science and Religion Series. Aldershot, England: Ashgate, 2002.

Wilken, Robert Louis. *Remembering the Christian Past*. Grand Rapids: Eerdmans Publishing Company, 1995.

Young, Robin Darling. "Cannibalism and Other Family Woes in Letter 55 of Evagrius of Pontus." In *The World of Early Egyptian Christianity: Language, Literature, and Social Context; Essays in Honor of David W. Johnson*, edited by James E. Goehring and Janet A. Timbie, 130–39. CUA Studies in Early Christianity. Washington DC: Catholic University of America Press, 2007.